Clerical Errors

A Comedy

Georgina Reid

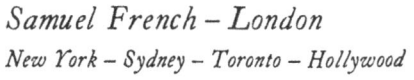
Samuel French – London
New York – Sydney – Toronto – Hollywood

Copyright © 1985 by Samuel French Ltd
All Rights Reserved

CLERICAL ERRORS is fully protected under the copyright laws of the British Commonwealth, including Canada, the United States of America, and all other countries of the Copyright Union. All rights, including professional and amateur stage productions, recitation, lecturing, public reading, motion picture, radio broadcasting, television and the rights of translation into foreign languages are strictly reserved.

ISBN 978-0-573-01608-0

www.samuelfrench.co.uk
www.samuelfrench.com

FOR AMATEUR PRODUCTION ENQUIRIES

UNITED KINGDOM AND WORLD
EXCLUDING NORTH AMERICA

plays@SamuelFrench-London.co.uk
020 7255 4302/01

Each title is subject to availability from Samuel French,
depending upon country of performance.

CAUTION: Professional and amateur producers are hereby warned that CLERICAL ERRORS is subject to a licensing fee. Publication of this play does not imply availability for performance. Both amateurs and professionals considering a production are strongly advised to apply to the appropriate agent before starting rehearsals, advertising, or booking a theatre. A licensing fee must be paid whether the title is presented for charity or gain and whether or not admission is charged.

The professional rights in this play are controlled by Samuel French Ltd, 52 Fitzroy Street, London, W1T 5JR

No one shall make any changes in this title for the purpose of production. No part of this book may be reproduced, stored in a retrieval system, or transmitted in any form, by any means, now known or yet to be invented, including mechanical, electronic, photocopying, recording, videotaping, or otherwise, without the prior written permission of the publisher. No one shall upload this title, or part of this title, to any social media websites.

The right of Georgina Reid to be identified as authors of this work has been asserted in accordance with Section 77 of the Copyright, Designs and Patents Act 1988.

CHARACTERS

Julie Briggs
Pete Briggs
Gran Briggs
James Martin
Mrs Martin
Sylvia Grey
Miss Pearson
Theodore Brown

The action of the play takes place in a disused Methodist Chapel

ACT I   SCENE 1   Early morning, December 1st
          SCENE 2   Later the same evening

ACT II   SCENE 1   A fortnight later, morning
           SCENE 2   The following Saturday afternoon

Time—the present

ACT I

Scene 1

A small disused Methodist Chapel. December 1st. Early morning

The chapel has not yet fallen into decay or disrepair, though the paint, walls and furniture are decidedly drab. There is no altar. On the central back wall we can read in letters of tarnished gold "Come Unto Him All Ye That Labour And Are Heavy Laden". Underneath this are two rows of choir stalls

To the right is a door to the vestry. To the left is a fairly plain pulpit with steps leading up to it. The offertory table has been pushed to one side, against the right wall. It has on it a small pile of hymn books, half a bottle of milk and a battered packet of cornflakes. There is a small pile of folding chairs against the left wall. Both right and left walls have a plain arched window

At the side front of the stage there are a few steps leading down into the auditorium and there is a pile of ancient kneelers near by, on the floor of the hall. The audience is in the position of the congregation

After a moment, the door opens and Sylvia, carrying a shopping bag, comes in with Mrs Martin. Sylvia, aged twenty-seven, is quite pretty and very determined whereas Mrs Martin is gentle, warm-hearted and middle-aged

Sylvia Heavens, it's cold in here!
Mrs Martin Yes, it always was a chilly building, even when the boiler was alight. I used to make James wear his thickest underwear when he was preaching here.
Sylvia (*smiling*) You spoil him. (*She sees the cornflakes and milk*) Good gracious, who's left their breakfast here?
Mrs Martin Breakfast? (*She sees the food*) That's very odd. Perhaps it's something left behind by the Sunday School.
Sylvia It's a bit thoughtless to dump it here, now the chapel is shut up. The milk will have gone bad and the food will attract mice. As soon as I've packed up these hymn books I'll take it away. (*She starts packing hymn books into the shopping bag*)
Mrs Martin (*looking around sadly and sighing*) What a strange, musty smell one finds in a place that's been shut up for weeks on end.
Sylvia Yes, damp and stale.
Mrs Martin It always used to smell of furniture polish and flowers. I feel very sad to see the place like this, unused and forgotten.

---

*N.B. Paragraph 3 on page ii of this Acting Edition regarding photocopying and video-recording should be carefully read.

Sylvia (*briskly*) It's been going downhill for years. If people won't come to chapel they must expect to see it closed down.

Mrs Martin James was very upset about it.

Sylvia Yes, I know. But at least he has more time now to give to his other chapels where he's more appreciated. Have you heard how soon you can move into the manse?

Mrs Martin The decorators hope to be out by the New Year. It'll be nice to be in our own place again. Furnished rooms never seem quite like home ... and there's simply nowhere for James to keep all his books.

Sylvia There ... that's all I can carry for the time being. (*She finishes packing up hymn books and picks up the cornflakes and milk*) I'll just get rid of this old junk——

Julie suddenly rears up from where she has been hiding in the pulpit. She is thin, scruffy and nearly eighteen. She wear jeans, an old jumper and a torn anorak

Julie 'Ere! You put that down!

Sylvia and Mrs Martin whirl round with a gasp

Sylvia I beg your pardon?

Julie Take your 'ands off that food!

Sylvia (*putting it down*) I had no idea ... please don't imagine I wanted it. I thought the place was empty.

Julie Well, it ain't.

Sylvia But it should be. It's been closed down. I mean ... what are you *doing* here?

Julie (*after a brief pause*) Prayin'.

Sylvia (*disbelieving her*) Praying?

Julie Yes, prayin'. That's what people do in church, innit?

Mrs Martin But ... you're in the pulpit.

Julie I know I am. The pulpit's the best place for prayin'. I tried them pews, (*she points to the audience*) but they was draughty.

Granny Briggs and Pete now show their heads above the choir stalls. She is sixty-five. He is sixteen. Both are unkempt and grubby

Mrs Martin Sylvia! There are more of them!

Sylvia (*to Gran and Pete*) Who are you?

They don't answer

(*To Julie*) What are *they* doing here?

Julie They're prayin' too.

Sylvia It didn't look as though they were praying. They were lying down.

Julie You can pray lying down can't you? God don't mind, does 'e? I bet God wouldn't mind if you was to pray standing on yer 'ead.

Mrs Martin It would hardly be reverent.

Sylvia Well, if you've finished praying I'll see you out and lock up behind you.

Julie I 'aven't finished. I've got a lot to pray about. Some people need more advice than others and I reckon I'll be 'ere for hours yet.
Sylvia (*very sweetly, but determined*) Look, I don't think you understand. This isn't the sort of chapel where people can come and go as they please. It's out of use. Closed down. I don't know how you got in but I'm afraid I must ask you to go.
Julie *You* must! Is it *your* chapel then?
Sylvia I'm engaged to the minister and this lady is his mother.
Julie I don't reckon that gives you the right to turn me out.
Sylvia But don't you see, you're trespassing.
Julie Trespassin'? When all I want is a quiet pray?
Sylvia (*picking up the cornflakes*) It looks more like a quiet picnic to me.
Julie (*angrily*) Put that food down. It's mine.
Sylvia (*to Mrs Martin*) Where's James?
Mrs Martin Outside, talking to Mr Brown.
Julie I'll fetch him. You keep an eye on things.

Sylvia exits R

Mrs Martin stands looking embarrassed

Pete, you get them cornflakes before somebody pinches 'em.

Pete emerges from the choir stalls. He is not by any means a half wit, but just a bit simple. He stands by the table, plunging his hand into the cornflakes and eating them dry

Gran Pass 'em round, lad. We're all 'ungry.

Pete offers the packet to Mrs Martin

Mrs Martin Er ... no thanks. I've already had breakfast.
Gran Don't waste 'em on 'er, Pete. Come and sit by Gran. Bring the bottle too.

Pete takes her the milk and the cornflakes

Julie Don't drink too much milk, Gran. We 'aven't got any more.
Pete Julie, that lady wants us to get out. Will we 'ave to go?
Julie (*determinedly*) No. We're stopping.
Pete That's good. It's nice 'ere.
Gran It's bloody cold.
Julie Never mind about cold. It's a roof over yer 'ead.
Pete Charlie likes it. I made 'im a little nest between two kneelers and 'e's as warm as toast. Do guinea-pigs like cornflakes? 'Ere, Charlie, 'ave some breakfast. (*He feeds the invisible guinea-pig in the stalls*)
Julie You better put Charlie back in 'is box for the time being. (*She peers out of the left window*)
Pete But Julie ...
Julie Do as I say. That woman's fetching the vicar. I can see 'em coming up the path.
Mrs Martin It's not the *vicar*. My son is a *Methodist* minister.

Julie What do I call 'im ... "your reverence"?
Gran They like you to call 'em "Father".
Mrs Martin No, no, simply call him Mr Martin. And I think you ought to come down out of that pulpit.
Julie No fear. I feel safer up 'ere. Now you two, keep quiet and leave the talking to me.

Sylvia enters R, *closely followed by James Martin, a pleasant-featured young man, muscular, healthy-looking, aged about thirty. He wears a dark suit with clerical vest and collar*

James (*jovial and fatherly*) Now then, young woman, what's this I hear?
Julie Well, *I* dunno what she told you, do I?
Mrs Martin They've been having their breakfast, James. And she won't get down from your pulpit because she says she feels safer up there.
James Yes, I know the feeling. When you're rather nervous, it's like a little fortress all round you. But there's no need to grip it like a drowning man. Nobody's going to hurt you, I promise you.
Julie (*glaring at Sylvia*) *She* wants to throw us out.
James I assure you, no-one will lay a finger on you, so why not come down and be introduced?
Julie I can be introduced from up 'ere. My name is Julie Briggs and this is my family. That's Gran and this 'ere is Pete.
James How do you do. My name is James Martin.
Julie I know. She told me.
James I am the minister in charge of this chapel. Don't you think you ought to have asked my permission, instead of walking in uninvited?
Julie I never knew people 'ad to be invited to go to church.
James How long have you been here?
Julie Since last night.
James How did you get in?
Julie We broke a window. I'm sorry. We was desperate.
Sylvia They're vagrants, James. Nothing but vagrants.
Gran Oh no, we ain't. You mind 'oo you're calling names.
Julie We're displaced persons.
James Where were you displaced *from*?
Julie Pike's Farm cottages. We was evicted.
James Evicted?
Mrs Martin Oh dear, how very unfortunate.
Sylvia (*with decision*) Leave this to me, James. I'll soon get this sorted out.

Sylvia exits R

James Look, I do wish you'd come down.
Julie Where's that woman gone? 'As she gone for the police?
James Of course not. Now, Miss ... er ... Briggs, what were you evicted for?
Julie Not paying the rent. We was three months in arrears.
James Three months! Good heavens, how did your parents fall so far behind?

Gran 'Aven't got no parents.
James You're an orphan?
Julie Course not. Me dad's in prison and me mum's . . . left 'ome.
Gran (*with venom*) She ran off with a bookie, the bitch. My son would tan the 'ide off 'er if 'e was 'ome.
Julie Gran, shurrup.
Gran Nasty, useless little trollop!
Julie Gran!

The old woman subsides and eats cornflakes

James And so there was no money coming in? Didn't you have a job?
Julie Yes, but I lost it. 'Ad to go on UB.
James UB?
Julie Unemployment Benefit. It ain't nearly enough.
James (*to Pete*) Well, what about you? Surely you've been earning something?

Pete cowers back, terrified. Julies rushes down the steps of the pulpit to come between Pete and James

Julie (*fiercely*) You leave 'im alone!
James I only asked if he'd been earning something.
Julie Don't you ask 'im nothing. Leave 'im alone. (*She turns to Pete and speaks more gently*) Pete, why don't you take Charlie outside for a bit of exercise? 'E could eat some grass in the graveyard.
Pete All right, Julie.

He picks up the shoe box containing the guinea-pig and hurries out R, cringing nervously as he passes James

James What's the matter with him? Did I frighten him?
Julie Everybody frightens 'im. 'E's very nervous and people scare 'im.
Gran 'E was always the same at school. Most of the time 'e was too scared to go. The attendance officer was always after 'im.
Julie 'E can't do a job, you see. 'E's not clever enough, and if somebody says something a bit sharp to 'im, like "'Urry up, you!" 'e starts to tremble and drop things, and the next day 'e won't go.
James And is he on UB too?
Julie No, 'e gets the Supplementary.
James And your Gran gets her pension?
Julie Huh. Never see that.
James Why not?
Julie Drinks it. (*She sees their disapproval*) Well, she's old, ain't she? She's not got much pleasure left in life. Why shouldn't she 'ave 'er drop of gin?
James So you never managed to pay the rent?
Julie Not very often. I tried to put away a bit every week, but it was no good. There was always somethink else cropped up. And we 'ad to eat, didn't we, and keep up the payments on the telly. In the end Mr Pike . . . the landlord . . . said 'is patience was exhausted and 'e was coming to put us out, tomorrow. Well, I wasn't going to wait for that and let the

neighbours see it 'appen, so last night, when it was dark, I brought 'em out of it.
Gran That's right, she brought us out of it—like Moses brought 'is people out of Egypt.
James Moses? (*He smiles wryly*) And you chose this as your Promised Land?
Julie Well, why not? (*She points upwards*) It says up there, "Come Unto 'Im, All Ye That Labour And Are 'Eavy Laden."
James (*gently*) I didn't think you'd done much labour lately.
Julie Well, any rate I was 'eavy laden, carrying that damn great suitcase all across the town. (*She indicates a battered suitcase standing, half hidden, behind the pulpit*)

James sighs and turns away in thought

(*To Mrs Martin*) I read in a book at school that even if you're a criminal they won't turn you away from a church. And we're not criminals, except for owing money.
Mrs Martin My dear, I feel terribly sorry for you but you can't think of living here. It would have to be deconsecrated.
Julie What's that? Like disinfected?
Mrs Martin No, no. But it's been blessed by the highest dignitary of the Methodist Church. It's sacred and must be used for holy things.
Julie But that's just the point. It ain't being used at *all*, is it? Is it?
Mrs Martin Well . . . no.
Julie Well, if no-one wants to use it for sacred things, why can't we use it to live in? (*She turns to James*) It'd only be for six months, till my Dad comes out of prison. We'd treat it proper, honestly. I'm sorry I broke that window. I'll stick a piece of cardboard over it.

During this speech, Sylvia has entered R

Sylvia (*to James*) It's all right, darling. I've fixed it. I rang the Social Services and they're sending someone right away.
Julie Oh! What did you go and do *that* for, you silly bitch?
James Now Miss Briggs, you'll do yourself no good with that kind of language.
Julie Well, what d'you think I went to all this trouble for? To get away from them welfare folk. Now they'll come and try to split us up.
Gran Don't let 'em split us up, your reverence. We've got to stay together.
Sylvia That may not be possible.
Julie We've got to. I promised our dad, when our mum left 'ome. I wrote and promised 'im.
Sylvia Surely your father would want what's best for you, even if it meant a temporary separation?
Julie No, no. Our Pete's got to sleep near me, else 'e gets nightmares. Mr Martin, can I speak to you on your own? It is your church, ain't it?
James Well, I'm the custodian, I suppose.
Julie Does that mean yes?
James Um . . . yes.

Act I, Scene 1

Julie Well then, I'd like to 'ave a private talk.
Sylvia (*decisively*) There's no need for that. Mr Martin is on his way to a meeting. If you'd like to go ahead, darling, I'll wait here until the Social Service Officer comes.
James I feel I ought to stay and see what can be done for these people. They've obviously been through a hard time and I'd like to ...
Syliva I know, dear, and you can safely leave it to me. You don't want to be late for the meeting, do you?
Julie That's right, you go and 'ave coffee and buns with the Mothers' Union. Don't you worry what 'appens to us. It's bugger you, Jack, I'm all right!
Sylvia (*coldly*) Please don't make a scene, Miss Briggs.
Julie Oh no, of course, it's common to make a scene, ain't it? Let a lot of selfish sods arrange your life and don't let on if it's breaking your 'eart, is that the way?
Gran Julie, Julie, that tongue of yours!
Julie Oh Gran, they aren't 'uman. They're s'posed to be religious but they just don't want to know.

Theodore Brown enters R. *He is a rather common, self-important man aged fifty*

Brown Ah, there you are, Reverend. Morning, Mrs Martin, morning, Miss Gray. Reverend, I really must protest ... am I interrupting something?
James What's the matter, Mr Brown?
Brown As you know, I was putting some flowers on my dear wife's grave. I come every week without fail, and have done since the day she was buried. No making do with everlasting flowers for my Dora.
Mrs Martin It does you great credit, Mr Brown.
Brown Thank you, Mrs Martin. Well, I'm bringing her this lovely bunch of chrysanthemums and what do I find? A great lout of a lad sitting on my Dora's grave, as comfortable as you please, boots up on the kerb, grinning like an idiot. I hastened towards him to remonstrate and what do you think? He had a guinea-pig there, eating my Dora's grass! Like a horrible ginger rat, it was.
Julie 'E's not 'orrible. 'E's a very nice guinea-pig.
Brown You know this ... this person then?
Julie That's my brother, Pete. 'E wouldn't do no 'arm to your wife's grave, just sitting on it.
Brown But it's sacrilege! Downright sacrilege! Isn't it, Mr Martin? And disrespect for the dead.
James Is he still there?
Brown No. As soon as I hollered at him, he picked up his guinea-pig and ran away. But the nerve of it! Whatever are we coming to that such things can happen?
Julie Pete don't understand about respect for the dead. 'E's a bit ... you know ... simple.
Brown Simple? I'll give him simple if I catch him!

James Er ... Mr Brown, this young lady is Miss Briggs and this is her grandmother.
Brown (*not impressed*) Oh yes?
James They have rather a problem. You see, the trouble is, they have nowhere to live.
Brown Oh? Since when?
James Since this morning. They have in fact been evicted through inability to pay the rent. I don't suppose you can think of any solution, can you?
Brown Solution? Well, they can't live with me, that's for sure. I have to keep my spare room handy for when my daughter comes to visit.
James Of course.
Mrs Martin And as you know, James and I are living in furnished rooms until the manse is ready for us to move in, so *we* can't help.
Sylvia And my brother's home from college, so *we're* full up.
Brown And in any case, you'll have trouble finding anyone willing to give house room to the likes of her.
Julie (*fiercely*) What do you mean, "the likes of me"?
James What are you implying, Mr Brown?
Brown Well, Reverend, you dwell above such matters, as it might be expected of one of your calling, but all the men of these parts know about *her*.
Julie They don't! That's a dirty lie!
Brown Look, young woman, I've seen you hanging about the pub, night after night, seeing who you could pick up. You can't deny it.
Gran She goes to the pub to buy me a bottle of stout. That's all it is. Our Julie's a good girl.
Julie Mr Martin, please don't listen to what 'e says. I'm not asking anyone to take us in, you know I'm not. All I want is your permission to let us stay in this building.
Brown What? Do my ears deceive me! You want to *live* in this sacred place? A girl of your reputation? Reverend, you're not considering letting her and the other two live in this *chapel*?
James The building is empty, Mr Brown ...
Brown Reverend, I beg to contradict you. With all respect, this dear old chapel may be closed down but it will never be empty while it is full of precious memories. Why, it was on this very spot that my dear wife and I were wedded. Are these down and outs to be allowed to sleep on such hallowed ground? In that font down there, (*he points above the heads of the audience*) my beloved children were christened. Is she to be allowed to wash her knickers in it?
Mrs Martin (*outraged*) Mr Brown!
Brown I beg your pardon, ladies, my feelings got the better of my good manners. But oh, Mr Martin, you wouldn't consent to such sacrilege, would you? If you did, every honest, chapel-going family in the town would rise up in outrage.
Sylvia Don't worry, Mr Brown, we've sent for the social worker and she'll sort it out to everyone's satisfaction.
Julie Not to mine, she won't. I wish I'd never come 'ere. I thought a church was a refuge. Summat about a present 'elp in time of trouble and all that.

Act I, Scene 1 9

James looks stricken

'Stead of which you're going to turn us out and separate us.
Mrs Martin You may not have to be separated. What about Mrs Beckett's boarding house?
Sylvia They'd never afford the rent.
Brown And in any case, Mrs Beckett keeps a *respectable* house.
Julie Ere! Just you . . .
James (*hastily*) Mr Brown, I wonder if I could talk to you about . . . about the choir practices at Flint Street Chapel. Perhaps we could go outside for a few minutes?
Brown Of course, Reverend. Did you want to change the night?
James I had wondered if it might be expedient . . .

James and Brown exit R, *talking together*

Mrs Martin I do wish the social worker would come. We're already late for the meeting.
Sylvia I wish James would go on without me. Quite honestly I think I could deal with this better without him.
Mrs Martin Why do you say that, dear?
Sylvia Well, I'm more practical than he is, don't you think? And he's putty in the hands of anyone with a hard luck story.
Mrs Martin Putty? I wouldn't say that. James can be quite firm when he makes up his mind.
Sylvia Then he'd better be firm this morning or Theodore Brown is going to rouse half the town in protest.
Julie (*sunk in gloom*) A pretty fine birthday this turned out to be.
Mrs Martin Oh, is it your birthday today? What a shame for you. We really must think of a place where you and your family could stay. Sylvia, do you think if I had a word with Mrs Beckett and reminded her . . .
Julie Don't bother. It wouldn't work. Even if we could afford the rent, she would never stand for . . . (*She glances at Gran who is eating cornflakes at the back, then goes and whispers in Mrs Martin's ear*)
Mrs Martin (*shocked*) Oh! (*She goes and whispers in Sylvia's ear*)
Sylvia (*turning and looking at Gran in distaste*) Oh no.
Julie Yes. That's 'ow it is, I'm afraid. (*She sits* DL, *biting her nails*)

James and Miss Pearson, a cheerful, business-like woman, enter R. *She is carrying a briefcase*

James This is Miss Pearson, the social worker.
Sylvia I'm glad to see you, Miss Pearson. I rang you because . . .
Miss Pearson (*gaily*) I know. I know. No need to say a word. I know Julie Briggs and her family. I've lived with 'em for years, you might say. Well, Julie, I never thought the day would come when I'd see you in church . . . and your Granny too. Where's Pete?
Julie Outside with Charlie.
Miss Pearson Good old Charlie! Now, you'd better do some explaining, young woman, because I've been on leave and only got back yesterday.

Julie Mr Pike was going to evict us so we got out last night and come 'ere.

Miss Pearson But . . . I thought Mr Pike said you could stay as long as you paid the rent.

Julie Yes . . . well, we 'adn't paid for weeks, see, 'cos we wanted the money for other things, and then Mr Pike said 'e wanted our cottage for the new man 'e was taking on.

Miss Pearson Oh, I wish I'd known. Something could have been arranged, if only there'd been time. Really, you know, it's not worth going on leave. One always comes back just in time to pick up the pieces. A month ago I had this case nicely worked out. Well, it's no use moaning. We've got some talking to do, so I don't think you ladies need stay. (*She urges them to the door*)

Sylvia Are you quite sure you can manage?

Miss Pearson Quite sure. Thank you for calling me. Don't *you* go, parson. I'd like you to stay and give me your advice. Good-morning, ladies. Shut the door as you go out, will you?

Sylvia and Mrs Martin exit R, *rather unwillingly*

Mrs Briggs, I take it you don't mind if the parson hears your case history?

Gran No, no. Let the 'oly father join the party.

James My name is Martin. James Martin.

Miss Pearson Right, Mr Martin. Now if you don't mind, let's have that table out, and some of these folding chairs, shall we? Things seem to sort out better if we sit round a table.

James helps her lift the table to C *stage, then while she opens her briefcase he helps Julie bring three folding chairs to the table*

Julie Come on, Gran, come and sit at the table.

Gran Is it dinner time?

Julie (*helping her to sit down*) No such luck.

Gran My stummick's rumbling like the very devil.

Julie So's mine. Pretend we're 'aving fish and chips, eh?

Gran Faggots and peas would be nice.

Julie You bet.

Gran and Miss Pearson sit, James remains standing. Julie is never at rest for long in any position, whether sitting, standing or leaning

James I'd like a few more details about this affair, if I may.

Miss Pearson Yes, of course. Their troubles began, as you can imagine, when Julie's father went into prison. You see, he worked on Pike's Farm and the cottage went with the job.

James Oh, a tied cottage?

Miss Pearson Exactly. There's not supposed to be such a thing any longer, but believe me, there is. Anyway, when Briggs was put inside, Mr Pike could reasonably have asked to have the cottage vacated, but he didn't want to be hard on them so he gave Julie's mother a job in the house,

Act I, Scene 1

looking after the children and doing a bit of housework, and let them stay on in the cottage. Well, unfortunately, last August Julie's mother left home.
Gran She ran off with a bookie, the bitch!
Miss Pearson Yes, quite. But Mr Pike, who has been remarkably humane I consider, said that as long as the rent was paid they could stay. Julie was out of work at the time, so I arranged for Supplementary Benefit to make them a weekly payment to cover the rent, and when I went on leave, all was peace and joy. What went wrong, Julie?
Julie Well ... I ... you see, I never *paid* the rent. I used the money for something else.
Miss Pearson Oh dear, what was it this time?
Julie A spin dryer.
Miss Pearson A spin dryer? What on earth ...?
Julie For Gran's sheets. I couldn't get them dry. It rained nearly every day and she was getting rheumaticks from damp sheets.
Miss Pearson Did you explain this to Mr Pike?
Julie (*unwillingly*) No. We 'ad a quarrel. 'E said things about our Pete.
Gran 'E never meant to be *rude*, exactly. 'E'd always got on well with our Pete, but 'e made a joke about 'im being gormless and ... well, you know our Julie.
Julie So we wasn't speaking to each other.
Gran And then Mr Pike got a new man to take over the tractors and things and 'e needed our cottage and 'e come round to tell us we'd 'ave to move and Julie threw a plant pot at 'im.
Miss Pearson Ye gods, Julie, it's a wonder you're not up in court.
Gran And a few days later we 'ad this letter telling us to be out by December 1st ... that's today ... on pain of eviction.
James I see. I suppose you can hardly blame Mr Pike. He seems to have given them every chance.
Miss Pearson They're certainly not ideal tenants. If they could hold down a job for more than a week it would be a help, but Pete's not really capable and Julie can't seem to keep a civil tongue in her head, so she gets the sack and back they go to social security.
Julie I was doing all right at my last job; I only lost it because I 'ad to go into 'ospital.
Miss Pearson Yes, well, I think we'd better give our first attention to getting your grandmother and your brother into suitable institutions, so that you can get another job.
Julie (*shrilly*) I knew it! I knew it! Mr Martin, don't let 'er do it, please don't let 'er send 'em into an 'ome! I promised my dad. Please Miss Pearson, let us stay on 'ere. It's my birthday. You can't do a thing like that on my birthday!
Miss Pearson (*firmly*) Sit down, Julie. I know for a fact that it's not your birthday for another fortnight. (*To James*) She always says it's her birthday when she sees disaster looming. The last time she tried it on was at the beginning of November. A neighbour threatened to sue them for enticing his dog away.

Julie We never enticed 'is dog away. It followed Pete 'ome. We couldn't get rid of it and it looked 'ungry so we give it some biscuits. ...

Miss Pearson Yes, yes, I know. I managed to pacify the dog's owner and having discovered that the dog had eaten the only food in the house I made them a cash payment of ten pounds ... not the first, I can assure you. How long did it last, Julie?

Julie (*sullenly*) I dunno. Can't remember.

Miss Pearson (*cheerfully*) I lay a bet it never lasted beyond Guy Fawkes Night. Am I right?

Julie Well, Pete loves fireworks.

Miss Pearson You see? They're totally improvident.

James How long will the father be in prison?

Miss Pearson Another six months. Now, what I have in mind for Pete, is the sheltered workshop just opening in Bessbury.

Julie What d'you mean, sheltered?

Miss Pearson A place where people like Pete can do simple work and earn a bit of money according to their ability, without the pressure of working for an employer or competing with more ... gifted people.

Julie It's not a loony-bin, is it?

Miss Pearson Certainly not.

Julie Where would 'e live?

Miss Pearson In a hostel adjoining the workshop.

Julie 'Ed 'ate it. 'E needs to live with me.

Miss Pearson He's a big boy of sixteen. You think of him as a child and that's bad for him. He'll be all right, you'll see. Now, your grandmother is rather more of a problem. We tried sending her to an old peoples' home when you were in hospital and it wasn't a success. There was quite a brawl, I believe, and Matron found gin bottles under the bed. (*She turns to James*) Added to this is the fact that she's incontinent, so no private home will take her in at the council's expense.

Julie (*standing up, her eyes blazing*) Stop it! Just you stop talking about my grandmother like that, telling a complete stranger all 'er secrets. Can't you realize that she's *ashamed* ... just like *you'd* be ashamed if I told a stranger that you wet the bed!

Miss Pearson Julie, stop shouting at me in that uncivilized manner. If you can't talk this over sensibly, kindly go and sit at the back of the church and leave me to settle the details with your grandmother.

Julie All right, I will. I'm not 'aving any more to say to you. You don't play fair. Just 'cos you know all our secrets, you think you can push us around as you please.

Julie flounces down the steps into the auditorium

Miss Pearson I'm only trying to bring some order into the chaos you've been living in.

Julie (*from the hall*) Don't you go telling 'im all my secrets, that's all. I'm warning you!

Julies goes to the back of the hall and sits

Act I, Scene 1   13

Miss Pearson Oh dear, we *are* prickly this morning. Sorry, Mrs Briggs. Didn't mean to hurt your feelings.
Gran That's all right, ducks. But I think I'll just slip outside if you'll excuse me. I shan't be long. (*She struggles to her feet*)
James (*opening the door for her*) Allow me.
Gran (*beaming*) Thank you, yer 'oliness.

Gran exits R

James (*smiling*) I've been promoted.
Miss Pearson Oh, she's an amiable old dear—when she's sober.
Julie (*from the back of the hall*) I 'eard that!
Miss Pearson We'd better wait until she comes back. I shall be needing her signature on a couple of papers.
Julie She's not signing anythink until I've read it and given my consent.
Miss Pearson I'm sorry, Julie, but until you're eighteen, you're only a child.
Julie (*jumping up*) A child? Look, I'm the only one in this family wot's got any sense at all!
Miss Pearson Nevertheless, legally you're a child.
Julie And you're an old fool!

Julie slams out at the rear of the hall

James She doesn't seem very grateful for all you're doing to help her.
Miss Pearson Mm, what do you expect? Gratitude is the most humiliating thing.
James All the same, she's a bit of a spitfire, isn't she?
Miss Pearson She's the pick of the bunch. She's held that family together until now, from sheer will-power. The old lady and the boy rely on Julie as head of the family and they're quite lost without her.
James Then isn't it a pity to separate them?
Miss Pearson A pity? It's a downright crime. It's the worst thing that could possibly happen to them, but what can I do? I've got to get a roof over their heads tonight, and there's no family accommodation available.
James How d'you think Pete will make out in this sheltered workshop?
Miss Pearson I shouldn't be surprised if he ran away the first night. He's a bad case of insecurity and I blame the mother for that. Poor Pete, he's better off without her. Julie's a better mother to him than she ever was.
James And Julie, what have you in mind for her?
Miss Pearson (*packing up her papers*) She can go and lodge with a neighbour until I can find something more permanent. Mrs Davies will have her, to help look after the babies. (*She rises*) Now look, I've got two more urgent cases to see before lunch and I can't wait for Granny Briggs any longer. I'll be back to pick them up about noon, will you tell them? Oh, and it would be a kind act if you could organize a cup of tea and a biscuit for them. They must be starving. You'll let them stay until I get back, I suppose? They've nowhere else to go, you know. Good-day, Mr Martin. Glad to have met you.

Miss Pearson exits R

Julie enters at the back of the hall and advances rather slowly up on to the stage where she stands, sad and defeated

Julie That Miss Pearson, I don't like 'er. She used to be a probation officer. Anyone 'ood bin in court 'ad to report to 'er once a week.
James Don't worry. She's gone.
Julie I know. But she's comin' back, I suppose?
James Yes. She's coming at noon.
Julie (*despairingly*) To take us away?
James Yes. (*After a pause*) But I'm not going to let her.
Julie What do you ... what do you mean?
James It's wrong to separate you. I want you to stay together here, in this chapel, until Miss Pearson can make better arrangements.
Julie Those other people'll be ever so angry ... Mr Brown and them ladies ...
James It doesn't matter. If I say you can stay, you can stay.
Julie (*staring dumbly at James for a moment*) I think I'm goin' to cry. (*She puts her hands over her face*)

James puts his arm round her and she weeps on his shoulder

CURTAIN

SCENE 2

The same. That evening

On the table stands a small camping gas stove, with a kettle on top. Gran and Julie sit at opposite ends of the table, sipping tea out of enamel mugs. They are relaxed with elbows on the table. There is not much light. Pete is sitting with his mug of tea at the foot of the steps, almost at hall level

Gran Them sausages was good.
Julie Yeh, smashing. I only burned 'em a little bit. See, I'm not used to this camping stove yet.
Gran Ain't it funny to think it all comes out of that little blue tin!
Julie Mr Martin says it's compressed gas.
Gran Compressed, is it! Fancy.

They sit in silence

 Sylvia enters R *and walks down to the front of the stage looking round expressionlessly*

Julie (*jumping up*) 'Allo.
Sylvia You're still here then?
Julie Yes. Mr Martin says we can.
Sylvia So I guessed.
Julie We was 'aving our tea. Would you like a cuppa?
Sylvia No thank you.

Act I, Scene 2   15

Pause

Julie I'm sorry I was rude to you this morning.
Sylvia (*very cool and discouraging*) It was nothing.
Julie I was all worked up.
Sylvia No doubt.
Julie I get worried you see, if I think we're going to be split up.
Sylvia What did the social worker say about your living here?
Julie Oh, she was tickled pink. It saves her the trouble of getting us somewhere else, dunnit?
Sylvia It's not so cold as it was.
Julie No. Mr Martin's lit the boiler. It took 'im ages and ages. I don't think 'e's used to that sort of work.
Sylvia Of course he isn't. He's a minister, not a caretaker. Where is he now?
Julie Gone to get some bulbs so we can 'ave a bit of light.
Sylvia The place smells.
Julie Oh. Well, we bin cooking sausages on that little stove. Mr Martin lent it to us.
Sylvia But . . . that's the offertory table!
Julie The what?
Sylvia The offertory table! Where the minister laid the offerings every Sunday!
Gran Well, we made a burnt offering. (*She cackles*)
Sylvia I don't think that's very funny. That table was almost like an altar. Mrs Martin made a beautiful embroidered cloth to go on it.
Julie What 'appened to it?
Sylvia It's in use at the Flint Street chapel.
Julie That's not closed down yet?
Sylvia Certainly not. It's a very flourishing chapel.
Julie Does Mr Martin preach there?
Sylvia Sometimes. Sometimes at Woodgrove Hill.
Julie I bet he preaches lovely. I bet all the chapel ladies are in love with 'im.
Sylvia Nonsense.
Julie I bet they are. If I was you I'd 'urry up and marry 'im. 'Ave you fixed the 'appy day?
Sylvia (*coldly*) I think perhaps your *own* plans for the future are of more concern, don't you?
Julie Oh, that's simple. We're stopping on 'ere until Miss Pearson can find us somethink better.
Sylvia Rent free?
Julie Of course.
Sylvia You're taking rather a lot for granted.

James enters R carrying two electric bulbs. He is now in slacks and a heavy jumper, which make him look younger and less dignified. He is without his dog collar. He looks cheerful and is obviously enjoying himself

James There you are, Julie. I've fixed a light in the vestry. (*To Sylvia*) Oh, hello darling.

Sylvia (*rather coolly*) Hello James.
Julie Come on, Gran. We can wash up now. Bring the kettle. (*She picks up the cups and saucers and moves towards the door*)

Gran follows with the kettle

James (*holding the door open*) The plug in the basin's not a very good fit, I'm afraid.
Julie I'll ram it in some'ow.

Julie and Gran exit

James I'll get you another tomorrow. (*He closes the door*) I could only get three bulbs. I had to purloin them from our own rooms. I think I'll put these two both at this end. The place is rather gloomy in the half light, isn't it? Hang on to this chair a minute, will you?

Sylvia holds the chair in silence as he mounts and fixes a bulb into a hanging socket, dismounts, moves the chair, remounts and fixes a second bulb into another socket

I hope they work. I haven't any more. (*He goes to the switch by the door and turns it on*) That's better. (*He dusts his hands on his trousers*) I'm filthy. I spent half the afternoon fighting with that pig of a boiler. If ever I go to hell fire I reckon I shall be made head stoker. Have they turned off the gas stove? Mustn't waste gas. Don't you think this was a brain wave? It's the camping stove that the Boy Scouts use.
Sylvia Does the Scoutmaster know that you've taken it?
James No, I must tell him tomorrow. He won't mind. I'll buy him a new cylinder of gas. (*After an embarrassed pause*) How did the meeting go, this morning?
Sylvia As you might expect, a bit flat. The ladies were disappointed when you didn't turn up. Mrs Christie had baked one of your favourite rum and chocolate cakes.
James Oh, have you brought it along? The Briggs family could use that.
Sylvia No doubt. Just like they could use anything that comes their way, so long as they don't have to pay for it.
James Sylvia . . . isn't that rather uncharitable?
Sylvia (*upset*) I consider that charity should go to deserving cases. I don't reckon these people *are*.
James Homeless people with nowhere to go?
Sylvia They had a home and they'd have it still if they'd paid the rent.
James But they hadn't enough money.
Sylvia Darling, that's nonsense. They did have money. Families like that, with the father in prison, get Supplementary Benefit to cover the rent. On top of that the girl gets unemployment benefit and the grandmother gets her old age pension. So what possible reason have they for getting themselves evicted? They're feckless and improvident.
James Hush. Pete can hear what you're saying.
Sylvia (*peering into the darkened hall*) I didn't see him, down there in the dark.

Act I, Scene 2 17

James Pete, I wonder if you would go out to my car and bring in everything you can find in the boot.
Pete Everything?
James Yes. With your strong arms, you'll probably manage the lot.

Pete grunts and mounts the steps, crosses and exits R

Now look, Sylvia, you may be quite right but they're not as well supplied with brains as you are. The old lady and the boy depend entirely on Julie and she's just a kid. Maybe she needs a few lessons in housekeeping.
Sylvia (*jealously*) And are you going to supply those too?
James Perhaps. Unless *you* feel inclined to help.
Sylvia I can't say I do. We don't speak the same language.
James No. I know what you mean.
Sylvia What does your mother think about this ... housing them in the chapel?
James She was a bit startled at first, but you know Mum. If I want a thing, it's all right with *her*, bless her.
Sylvia Yes. (*Sadly*) I wish I were a bit more like that, don't you? Happy to accept a thing, just because you want it?
James (*putting his arms round her with a smile*) No, I like you as you are; strong-minded, domineering and upright as a telegraph pole.
Sylvia What sort of marriage are we going to have if we can't see eye to eye?
James We'll work things out as they come along. If you don't approve of what I'm doing, I can't make you. But I must go ahead with it because ... well ...
Sylvia Well, why?
James Did you hear what the girl said? A half-remembered phrase from her schooldays. ... "God is our refuge and strength. A very present help in time of trouble."
Sylvia (*breaking away from him*) At least you don't have to *enjoy* it so much.
James (*surprised*) Enjoy it?
Sylvia You're enjoying every minute of it. It's exciting. It's like a jolly game you're organizing for the Sunday School Christmas party. Only this game won't turn out to be so jolly, you'll find. There won't be a prize for the winner or a round of applause for the funniest hat!

Julie enters R *and holds open the door for Pete, who is laden with blankets, sleeping bags and a ground sheet*

Julie Pete said you told 'im to bring these in. Is it all right?
James Yes, quite all right. Sylvia ...
Sylvia (*going*) There's not much point in my staying. I never was much good at party games. Good-night James.
James Sylvia, won't you ...?

Sylvia exits R *out and shuts the door firmly*

Julie What did she mean, party games?
James She thinks I'm doing this for a bit of excitement. She says I'm enjoying it.

Julie Well, I suppose in a way it makes a change for you. A bit different from sitting by old ladies' bedsides or opening church bazaars.
James Is that what you think I do all the time?

Between them, they gradually unload Pete and pile the things at L *as they talk*

Julie I dunno. What *do* you do all the time?
James Well, this week, besides preparing and preaching two sermons, I've performed one funeral and two christenings, made up the circuit accounts, presided at the Mens' Fellowship, taken a choir practice because the choirmaster was ill, visited several patients in hospital and done three hours' work on the quarterly plan. Oh, and had a rather pointless committee meeting.
Julie It doesn't sound very interesting.
James No, but it's necessary.
Julie Is it? I dunno.
James (*nonplussed*) Don't know if it's necessary?
Julie Well, when you come to think of it, it wouldn't 'ave mattered very much if you 'adn't done *any* of those things really—except for the funeral. I reckon what you're doing now is far more necessary, don't you?
James (*grinning*) Yes, as a matter of fact, I do. Now, let's get your sleeping quarters organized. We'll shift this table first of all.

They move the table

I got hold of these sleeping-bags from the Scout Hut, and a couple of blankets, and I thought if we made a sort of mattress of kneelers, it wouldn't be too hard on the floor.
Julie That's a wonderful idea. Pete, can you go down and fetch that big pile of kneelers?

Pete goes down the steps to the pile of kneelers

We'll lay them out here and ... oh, what about Gran? She can't sleep in a sleeping bag in case ... you know.
James I've brought a rubber ground sheet for Gran. She can have blankets on top, cotton sheets below. How's that?
Julie Wonderful. And if she 'as an accident I'll wash 'er sheets and dry 'em in the graveyard on Dora's tombstone.
James (*laughing*) You certainly won't. First thing tomorrow I'm going round to Farmer Pike and get back your spin dryer. There's a power point in the vestry.

He takes the kneelers that Pete is piling on the edge of the stage and passes them two by two to Julie who kneels in the centre and makes them into a big mattress, (eighteen kneelers) and a smaller one for Gran (ten kneelers)

Julie Ain't it wonderful? You know, you're like one of them conjurors the way you make things 'appen.
James Just a bit of organization, that's all that's needed.
Julie Yeh, I know. That's what I used to tell myself, but it didn't work

Act I, Scene 2 19

some'ow. I'd organize the rent money every week, but it was always needed for summink else.
James Like fireworks, for instance?
Julie (*pausing in her task*) Oh, I know you think that was awful, but we really needed them fireworks. We was all so fed up and missing our dad. So I blued the rent . . . see?
James Yes, I do understand. One crowded hour of glorious life, eh?
Julie You bet. Better'n the telly, it was.

As they talk they lay out the ground sheet, the cotton sheets and blankets and two sleeping bags

James You managed to keep the television then?
Julie No, they fetched it away last September. We don't arf miss it during the dark evenings.
James Is that why you started hanging round the pubs?
Julie (*embarrassed*) No. I 'ad to do that. I didn't want to.
James You mean, your grandmother sent you?
Julie No, it was my own idea. I wanted the money and all the girls said that the soldiers paid well.
James Paid well for what?
Julie (*with a look*) You know.
James (*aghast*) Julie!
Julie Pete, go and see if Gran needs you, there's a love.

Pete exits R

James So what Mr Brown said about you was right.
Julie Not any more it isn't. I only did it for the money and I didn't enjoy it at all.
James Did your grandmother know?
Julie Not until later. It was because of 'er I wanted the money. I 'ad to bail 'er out for being drunk and disorderly. I didn't see 'ow else I could get the money quickly, see? (*Earnestly*) I was only selling somefink what was mine to sell. It wasn't dishonest, like stealing.
James But Julie . . . the risks you ran!
Julie Don't I know it! I got pregnant in no time, in spite of doing everythink my friends told me.

Her tone is quite matter of fact, neither proud nor ashamed of herself. James stares at her, robbed of speech

> That's why I 'ad to go into 'ospital. The doctor didn't argue nor nothink. 'E said it would be wrong to bring another child into our family under the circumstances. And so I lost my job and Gran and Pete caused any amount of trouble . . . so you don't need to worry, Mr Martin. I shan't do *that* again. I can't see why people do it at all. It's 'orrible. All the girls at school were dead keen, I can't think why.

James All the girls at school?
Julie Yes. They look down on you if you're fifteen years old and still a virgin.

James But at fifteen you're still a child!
Julie Not where I come from you ain't. Oh, Mr Martin, you just don't know about people like us. I expect if you 'ad known—if I'd told you this morning what I told you just now—you'd never 'ave let us stay 'ere, would you?

James is silent

Does this mean we'll have to go?
James (*decisively*) No. (*He kneels beside her, arranging blankets*) I was ... startled, that's all. But I'd be a pretty poor sort of minister if I didn't want to help you still.
Julie All the same, I've spoiled your little game, 'aven't I?
James What little game?
Julie Like your sweetheart said, you was all starry-eyed at your clever scheme to help poor 'omeless people. But *she* knew the sort we are, all right.
James The sort you are? You're no different from the rest of us, Julie. We're all one family.
Julie (*vehemently*) Oh no, we ain't. There's your kind of family and there's my kind. You don't know what it's like to be 'ungry, you've never come 'ome and found your mother 'ad run off with a bookie, you've never 'ad to put your gran to bed blind drunk. You want to try it for yourself, then you'd know what you was talking about!

James stands, rather hurt and taken aback, while Julie shakes sleeping bags vigorously

Pete enters R, *followed by Gran*

Pete 'Ere, Julie, Gran says there ain't no street lights outside the window. Is that true?
Julie Yes, of course it is.
Gran 'E's afraid it'll be dark when 'e goes to bed.
Julie Well, it may be a bit darker than wot you're used to, but Gran and I'll be right 'ere beside you. Look, Pete, you're going to 'ave a sleeping bag, just like the boy scouts use.
Pete (*thrilled*) Am I? When can I go to bed?
Julie Well, it's a bit early. What time is it, Mr Martin?
James Nearly nine o'clock.
Gran I know it's early, Julie, but I'm ready to drop. I never slept a wink last night, and I've got the rheumaticks in my legs.
Julie All right, let's 'ave an early night then. I'm sleepy too.
James In that case, I'll say good-night. Is there anything else I can get you?
Julie No thanks, Mr Martin. Everythink's wonderful. I am grateful, honest, even though I don't sound like it.
James (*still a little hurt*) I hope you all sleep well. Here's the key of the back door. You can lock up after I've gone.
Julie (*taking the key*) What about the front door?
James It's locked. I keep the key to that. What time do you have breakfast?

Julie I dunno. Depends when I wake up.
James Well, don't try to light the stove until I get here. I'll come about eight.
Julie OK.
James Good-night, Mrs Briggs.
Gran Good-night, your worship.
James Good-night, Pete.
Pete (*busy peering into a sleeping-bag*) Night.

James opens the door for Julie and they go out

Gran sits heavily in chair L. Pete puts his head right to the bottom of the bag and does a forward roll across the mattress of kneelers. He emerges, laughing.

Pete Did you see that, Gran?
Gran Yes luv, I saw yer.
Pete These bags are like they use for sack races.

Julie enters R

Julie, we could 'ave a sack race with these bags. I bet I could win you. . . .
Julie (*sharply*) You'll do nothing of the sort. You gotta take care of that bag. It don't belong to us. (*She crosses to the suitcase behind the pulpit and takes out a towel and pair of pyjamas, both rather grubby*) 'Ere you are, go and 'ave a wash in the vestry and get into yer pyjamas.
Pete Do I 'ave to wash?
Julie Yes, you do.
Pete Why?
Julie 'Cos this is a church, that's why.
Pete Oh, all right.

Pete exits R, unwillingly

Gran I 'ad a wash after we done the pots, Julie.
Julie You'll do then, but yer 'air's a mess. (*She goes to the suitcase*) 'Ere's the comb, and 'ere's yer nightie. Can you manage yer undressing?
Gran Wot . . . 'ere?
Julie Of course. Nobody can see you.
Gran It don't seem right, undressing in a church.
Julie You gotta forget it's a church.
Gran 'Ow can I with them rows of pews looking at me? I think I'll go be'ind the pulpit. It's more private.
Julie Please yourself.

Gran goes behind the pulpit and takes off her jumper, then puts on a voluminous nightie and wriggles out of her underclothes beneath its cover

Gran Am I going in a sleeping-bag too?
Julie No, Mr Martin's got a groundsheet and some blankets for you.
Gran 'E's a gent is Mr Martin.
Julie Yeh.
Gran 'Ave you told 'im?

Julie What?
Gran About the baby.
Julie Yeh.
Gran What's 'e say?
Julie Not much. Turned a bit quiet though. I reckon 'e was shocked.
Gran Yeh, 'e would be.

Pete enters R carrying a towel, dressed in pyjamas

Pete That water was as cold as ice, Julie.
Julie Pooh, don't be a cissy.
Pete I bet *you* won't wash in it.
Julie Yes I will. Gimme the towel.

Julie grabs the towel and marches out R

Gran emerges from behind the pulpit

Pete I'm getting into bed.
Gran Take yer shoes off then.
Pete Can I keep my socks on?
Gran Why not? Pretend it's bed socks.

Pete leaps on to the mattress and wriggles into a sleeping-bag. Gran sits, takes the pins from her hair and combs it

Pete It's lovely and warm in this 'ere bag. Can you zip me up, Gran?
Gran I doubt if I can bend down that far, luv. You better wait till Julie gets back.
Pete I 'ope she won't be long coming. I get a bit nervous at night if I don't know where she is. (*After a pause he suddenly sits up*) Gran! Where's Charlie?
Gran I dunno, luv. In 'is box, I suppose. Where's that?
Pete Ain't it there on the table?
Gran No.
Pete (*anxiously*) 'E's got away then. 'E's running loose in the church.
Gran Well, never mind. 'E can't come to no 'arm, can 'e?
Pete But 'e'll be frightened. I'll 'ave to find 'im. (*He scrambles out of the sleeping-bag*)
Gran Ain't you never going to settle down?

Pete, in his stockinged feet, goes down to the foot of the steps and peers round nervously

Pete Charlie! 'Ere, Charlie! Where are you, boy?
Gran 'Ave you got 'im?
Pete No. It's dark down 'ere and I can't see.
Gran P'raps 'e's gone down a mouse 'ole.
Pete No, 'e's too big for that. Oh, I remember now! I left 'is box be'ind the pulpit. (*He retrieves the shoe box from behind the pulpit*) I've got 'im, Gran. 'E's just where I left 'im. (*He moves back to his sleeping-bag, speaking words of love to his guinea-pig in its shoe box*) Poor old Charlie,

Act I, Scene 2

left in a corner all by yourself. Were you frightened, boy? It's all right now, Daddy's got you. You'll be all right now.
Gran Put 'im on the table then.
Pete No, 'e's going to sleep next to me, then 'e won't be frightened in the dark. (*He sits on the mattress, stroking the guinea-pig in the box*) Are you comfy, old chap? Got enough straw to keep you warm?
Gran The way you talk to that animal, anyone'd think it was ... Aaaaaaaah! (*She gives a shrill scream as she looks toward the window,* R)
Pete (*frightened*) What's up?
Gran A face! I saw a face at the window!
Pete Gran, you never!

Julie runs in looking anxious, towel in hand

Gran I tell you I did. There's someone out there, looking in at us!
Pete It's one of them dead people, come up out of the grave!
Julie Gran, you didn't really see a face, did you?
Gran Yes I did. A nasty, white evil face, staring in at me. 'Orrible.
Julie Shurrup, Gran. You'll frighten Pete.
Gran (*soberly*) I didn't imagine it, Julie. It *was* there.
Julie Well, it's not there now. 'Ere, put this blanket round you. You're shivering. (*She takes a blanket from the bed and puts it round Gran*)
Gran What d'you think it was?
Julie Probably yer own reflection. Why should anyone want to look at you in yer nightdress, eh? (*Laughing*) Still 'oping, are yer?
Gran Get on with yer, sauce box.
Julie Let's all 'urry up and get into bed and 'ave a bit of shut-eye. Where's my nightie?

Pete climbs into his sleeping bag. Julie takes a cheap, pretty nightie out of the suitcase. She turns her back, pulls off her jumper and puts on the nightie over her jeans

Julie (*as she changes*) Cor, it's damn cold, innit? I 'ope we get a better night's sleep than we did last night. I think that was the longest night I've ever lived through.
Gran You're not goin' to bed in them trousers are yer?
Julie Dunno. I might. This nightie wasn't built for warmth.
Gran I wish we 'ad some curtains we could draw.
Julie Look, you gotta stop wanting things like that. We're jolly lucky to ...
(*She gasps as she sees the door open* R)

Theodore Brown enters R

'Ow did *you* get in?
Brown Through the door.
Julie But I locked it.
Brown I've got my own key. I used to be society steward for this chapel.
Julie What d'you want? We was just going to bed.
Gran (*suddenly*) It was *you* what looked in the window at me!
Julie *Was* it?

Brown I may have glanced in as I passed.
Julie You frightened my grandmother out of 'er wits and Pete thought it was a ghost.
Brown Well, what a nervy lot you are. (*He looks round*) So, you're all ready for bed, are you?
Julie Mr Martin says we can stay.
Brown Ah well, Mr Martin carries Christian kindness a bit too far in my opinion. However, if he wants to make himself unpopular I mustn't interfere. Sleeping-bags, eh? Whose are those?
Julie Boy scouts'.
Brown Oh, ah. And a mattress of kneelers. Well, I hope you'll sleep comfortably. It wouldn't do for me. Too hard and draughty. I've got a very nice bed at my house, Julie. It's a double bed and it's got a spring mattress and soft feather pillows and a big fat eiderdown *and* an electric blanket.
Julie What are you telling *me* for?

Brown shrugs and laughs

> *James enters silently at the back of the hall, unobserved. He wears a sports jacket over his pullover and carries a red roadside lantern. He advances quietly and stands in the shadows at one side*

Brown Have you had your supper then?
Julie Yes, thanks. Mr Martin brought us some sausages.
Brown Oh, very kind. And has he provided breakfast too?
Julie We've got some bread and some tea.
Brown Bread and tea! Prison fare! I could let you have some eggs and a few nice rashers of bacon from the shop—and some best quality coffee.
Gran We ain't got no money to pay for 'em.
Brown No need to pay. I'm not hard up.
Gran This is a change of 'eart, innit? This morning you said ...
Brown Oh, this morning. Forget what I said this morning. My tongue runs away with me sometimes. But I wouldn't see you go hungry. I'll let you have a few groceries any time Julie likes to come over and ask for them.
Julie Oh. Well, thanks. I'll pop over in the morning.
Brown Why wait till morning? You can pop over now.
Julie I'm not properly dressed ...
Brown I don't mind that. Come on, put your coat on before I change my mind.

Julie gets her anorak from the choir stalls and puts it on

Pete Julie, you won't be long, will you? I don't like it without you.
Brown You're a bit big to be afraid of the dark, aren't you? I'd be ashamed to talk like that at your age.
Gran It's all right, Pete. I'll be 'ere.
Brown That's right, your granny'll be here to hold your hand and tomorrow morning Julie'll bring you some nice eggs and bacon.
Julie (*startled*) Tomorrow morning?

Act I, Scene 2   25

Brown Come along then. It's only across the street.
Julie (*removing her anorak*) I'm not coming. You never said I was to stay the night.
Brown Well, I thought you understood. It's not a bad bargain, is it, a nice warm bed and a box of groceries, a couple of times a week?
Julie You can keep your groceries and stuff them! I wouldn't sleep with you, not if I was starving!
Gran You dirty old man!
Brown You keep out of this. Your granddaughter isn't so hard to get, from what I hear.
Julie I've finished with all that.
Brown Think I believe that? Once a whore, always a whore.
Julie Get out of 'ere and take your dirty talk with you!
Brown Oh no, I'm not going unless you come with me.
Julie I told you, I'm not coming.
Gran After what you just called 'er? You must be mad.
Brown I'm not mad and I'll tell you why she'll come. Because if she doesn't, I'm going to write to the President and tell him what's going on behind his back.
Gran The President?
Brown The Methodist President. The Reverend Martin's employer. And when he finds out what's going on here, your precious Mr Martin'll get the sack.
Julie (*horrified*) You wouldn't do such a thing!
Brown I wouldn't *like* doing it. I'd much rather leave things as they are. A pleasant little arrangement like the one I just mentioned would suit us all very nicely. (*He advances, smirking*)

Julie stares at him, petrified

You look very pretty in that nightie, Julie. I can see why the soldiers were so keen on you.
Julie Don't you touch me!
Brown Who's going to stop me? Your granny?
James (*putting down the lantern*) I am!

James leaps up on to the stage and gives Brown a vigorous push which nearly overthrows him

Keep your hands off that girl!
Brown You assaulted me! A minister of the church and you assaulted me!
James I haven't assaulted you yet but I will if you ever touch that girl again.
Brown (*blustering*) She didn't mind. She asked for it.
Julie I never. 'E wanted me to go to 'is 'ouse and spend the night.
Brown You brazen little liar! I was going to give you some groceries.
Julie And a lot more besides!
James (*loudly*) That's enough! I know exactly what you suggested to that girl, Mr Brown. I've been listening to you for the past five minutes and I'm appalled at what I heard.
Brown There's no need to take that attitude, Mr Martin. Even *you* must

realize that when a man's a widower he can't live like a monk for the rest of his life. I was doing that girl a favour.

James Brown, you disgust me. The sooner you leave this building the better.

Brown While you stay here and put her to bed, I suppose?

James (*seizing him and propelling him to the door*) You nasty piece of work! Get out of here before I do you an injury!

James thrusts the spluttering Brown out of the door R *and beyond*

Gran puts her arm comfortingly around Julie

The outer door bangs and James returns, still angry

That's the first time I've wanted to hit a man and hurt him. I've not been nearer to a stand up fight since I left school. I feel quite exhilarated.

Gran You was wonderful, Mr Martin. You was like the 'ero of a film!

Julie Will 'e really tell the President?

James It won't make any difference if he does. I wrote to the President myself, this afternoon, and made the situation clear. I shall be very surprised if I get more than a gentle reprimand.

Julie You ought to get a medal, coming to the rescue like that. What made you come back?

James I brought a lantern for Pete. Where have I left it? (*He goes down the steps and fetches the lantern*) It's so that the place won't seem so dark when the lights are out. Look, Pete, it's like the workmen leave by the roadside when they've dug a hole and don't want you to fall in.

Pete What makes it red?

James It's red glass, you see. Just an ordinary oil lamp with red glass.

Pete It's better 'n a night light, innit?

James Much better. Julie, how did that man get in? Did you let him in?

Julie No fear. 'E 'ad a key of 'is own. Oh Gawd, 'e might come back after you've gone!

James Don't worry, I'm not going.

They stare at him

Julie Not going?

James No. I've been thinking about what you said, Julie.

Gran What did she say?

James She said I had no right to say we're all members of one family until I'd tried living *your* way. Isn't that what you said, Julie?

Julie (*upset*) Look, I was rude. Bloody rude.

James No, no, it was absolutely true. And I want to find out what happens to people like you ... by living with you, if you'll let me.

Gran Live 'ere in the chapel, just like us?

James That's right. Could you sort of pretend that I was your son, Mrs Briggs? Julie's father?

Gran Well, you're not much like Frank, but still ... it would be a comfort to 'ave you. What d'you think, Julie?

Act I, Scene 2   27

Julie But you wouldn't like it, Mr Martin. You'd 'ate it. It's awful, the way we live, compared to the way *you* live.
James If it is, then I want to find out. I've come prepared to stay if you'll have me.
Julie What about your mother?
James I've written her a letter. She'll find it tomorrow morning.
Julie And your sweet'eart, 'ave you written to 'er?
James No. I'll have to try and explain it to her. It won't be easy.
Julie You won't stick it for long, I bet you anythink.
James We shall see, shan't we? (*He looks pleased and excited*) So, I'll stay, shall I? Where shall I sleep? Is there a spare sleeping-bag? Do you want me to go out in the vestry?
Pete (*definitely*) No. You stay in 'ere with us.
Gran I doubt if this mattress'll take more than two.
James I'll lay out some more kneelers over here, then. (*He goes to the pile of kneelers that Pete has left in a corner of the stage*)
Julie No. Put them up there in the pulpit.
James (*doubtfully*) In the pulpit? I don't think I'd fit.
Julie No, but I would. I always curl up small. It'd be like my own little bedroom, all private and cosy and safe.
James Safe? All right, Julie, you shall have your safe little bedroom and I'll sleep down here, next to Pete.
Julie (*going up into the pulpit*) Pass up the kneelers then.

James goes to and fro, carrying several kneelers at a time until she has received and laid down about eight. As they work they talk. Gran gets into bed upstage of Pete

James You'll have a nice cosy little nest up there.
Julie This morning you said it was like a little fortress.
James What was?
Julie This pulpit.
James Well, so it is, in a way. You'll be like a princess in a tower. My mother used to tell me a story about a princess in a tower. Rapunzel, her name was.
Julie What an awful name.
James It is, rather, isn't it? Anyway, Rapunzel had long golden hair, so long that when she leaned out of the window her hair reached right down to the ground and her lover used to climb up it when he came to visit her.
Julie The stuff they tell kids! Can you spare me a blanket?
James Yes, you take this blanket and I'll take the sleeping-bag.
Julie OK.
James Now, is everybody in bed? How about you, Gran? Are you comfortable? (*He kneels to tuck her in*)
Gran Snug as a bug dearie, thanks.
James That's good, Pete? You all right?
Pete Yeh.
James Charlie all right?
Pete Yeh.

James puts out the lights. The stage is lit by the red glow of the lantern

(*Raising his head*) Look Gran, it gives a lovely red light. Don't it make the place look cosy?
Gran Yes luv. Now go to sleep.

Pete lies down. James, who has taken off his jacket and shoes, climbs into his sleeping-bag next to Pete, facing the other way. He remains sitting up, looks round for a moment, then rests his head on his arms and knees in a very relaxed manner. Julie peers down at him, puzzled

Julie (*after a moment*) What are you doing?
James (*looking up with a smile*) Just reporting to my Probation Officer.
Julie Oh. Sorry I interrupted you.
James That's all right. Finished now. Go to bed. (*He lies down*)

Julie disappears from view

Good-night, family.
All Good-night.

CURTAIN

ACT II

SCENE 1

The same. A fortnight later

A clothes line has been strung across the rear alcove and a rather tatty sheet is hanging from it, almost obscuring the choir stalls. Some towels are hanging over the pulpit sides. The kneelers and bedding are out of sight and the table has been brought forward again

Pete is busy fixing a large poster to the pulpit with a hammer and nails. The poster depicts St Francis, barefoot, clad in a long shift and carrying a staff, surrounded by birds and animals

Mrs Martin enters R. *carrying an umbrella over her arm. She looks round in amazement*

Pete has stopped hammering and is admiring his handiwork. When Mrs Martin starts to speak he is startled, but her manner is so gentle that he recovers his confidence quite soon

Mrs Martin Hello. I'm looking for Mr Martin. Is he here?
Pete (*with a gulp*) No.
Mrs Martin Oh, he's gone out, has he?
Pete Yeh. They're all out, 'cept me.
Mrs Martin Do you know when he'll be back?
Pete Soon. Yeh, that's right. 'E'll be back soon.
Mrs Martin In that case, I'd better wait. I don't want to have to come back after lunch.
Pete You can sit down. I bin dusting them chairs.
Mrs Martin Have you really? That was a kind thought. (*She sits* R)
Pete I didn't *think* of it exactly. 'E *told* me to do it. 'E said I'd get no dinner if I didn't do summat to earn it. I dusted all them pews too. They was filthy.
Mrs Martin Yes, they must have been due for a dusting. And now you're putting up a picture I see.
Pete Yes. It's Jesus. I found it out there, (*he nods towards the vestry*) all rolled up in a corner, getting dirty. Mr Martin said I could put it up 'ere.
Mrs Martin Did he say you could nail it to the pulpit?
Pete Yeh. 'E said it was full of worm 'oles already, so a few more 'oles wouldn't matter.
Mrs Martin That picture used to hang in the Sunday School. The little ones all liked it very much.
Pete Yeh. It's nice. All them animals.

Mrs Martin It's not Jesus, you know.
Pete Innit?
Mrs Martin No, it's St Francis.
Pete Oo?
Mrs Martin St Francis of Assisi. He was a young man of noble family who lived in Italy.
Pete It's 'ot in Italy.
Mrs Martin Yes, hot sunshine and beautiful blue skies. Francis could have lived in a splendid palace and had lots of servants, but he preferred to live in the fields with all the birds and animals. He used to call them his little brothers and sisters.
Pete (*impressed*) Caw!
Mrs Martin (*obviously back in the Sunday School*) All he had to eat was the dry bread that people threw away, but he always shared it with the animals. They used to follow him about. He couldn't bear to see them ill-treated, so he travelled up and down the country, setting them free.
Pete I let Charlie go free in the churchyard, every morning.
Mrs Martin That's right.
Pete Did this Francis like guinea-pigs?
Mrs Martin *All* God's creatures.
Pete I don't see no guinea-pigs in the picture. (*He goes and looks at the poster closely*)
Mrs Martin Are you sure?
Pete Per'aps there's one be'ind this rabbit, only we can't see it 'cos the rabbit's so fat.
Mrs Martin Ah. That's probably right.
Pete I 'ad a rabbit once. I 'ad it for two years and then, one day ...

Sylvia enters R

(*He breaks off and looks uneasily at Sylvia*) I gotta go and peel some potatoes. Mr Martin said I better do six if they wasn't too big.

Pete exits R

Sylvia stands aside rather markedly as he passes

Sylvia (*coming downstage*) Where's James? Is he not back yet?
Mrs Martin No. I'm waiting for him.
Sylvia Look at this place! It's more like a Chinese laundry than a chapel.
Mrs Martin Yes, I'm just hoping that none of the Women's Circle looks in and sees it.
Sylvia I don't know. It might reassure them that James isn't living in some cosy little love nest.
Mrs Martin Love nest?
Sylvia Well, that's what Mrs Partridge seems to think.

As Sylvia talks she keeps busy taking down and folding the sheets on the line and generally tidying up. Mrs Martin helps her

She stopped me in town this morning and asked me if it's true that James has thrown me over and gone to live with a woman of easy virtue!

Act II, Scene 1   31

Mrs Martin Oh no!
Sylvia Theodore Brown must have been spreading tales. Naturally I set her straight. I told her the absolute truth ... but the truth is very nearly as awful. Mrs Martin, whatever has come over James? Has he ever done anything like this before?
Mrs Martin Well, once, when he was very small, he brought some gypsies home to tea. Apart from that he's always been very respectable.
Sylvia Respectable? That would hardly describe him now. Yesterday, he and that gormless boy were sitting in the park, side by side, eating chips out of a newspaper! And Mr Curtis at the bank said that when James came in to draw out some money, he hardly recognized him. He hadn't shaved for days!
Mrs Martin Oh dear, and Mr Curtis is on the Committee. I really must speak to James when I see him.
Sylvia (*grimly*) I've seen him.
Mrs Martin Today?
Sylvia Yes, this morning. In the Post Office.
Mrs Martin What did he say?
Sylvia He didn't see me. He was having a set to with the old lady.
Mrs Martin A set to?
Sylvia Yes, a full-scale row with Granny Briggs, right there in front of everybody.
Mrs Martin But, that's so unlike James.
Sylvia Well, to do him justice, he was as quiet and reasonable as always, but she was being shockingly loud and common. I heard her call him a ... a bloody thief ... and she used words that I couldn't repeat. Everyone was most embarrassed.
Mrs Martin Oh, poor James!
Sylvia Poor James? In my opinion he's enjoying every minute of it.

Sound of the outer door opening

Mrs Martin Hark. I think he's coming.

James enters R, *coughing. He looks rather pale and unshaven. He carries a laden shopping bag. Pete follows him and closes the door*

James Hallo, Mother. Hallo, Sylvia. Looking for me? (*He has a spasm of coughing*)
Mrs Martin James, that's a dreadful cold.
James Don't worry, Mother. It's not as bad as it sounds. (*He takes off his jacket and shakes it*)
Mrs Martin And your coat! It's wet through!
James I know. I've been out shopping. (*He puts his jacket on the clothes horse*) Spent all our money, I'm afraid.
Sylvia Are they supporting you out of National Assistance?
James Certainly not. I contribute the equivalent of Unemployment Benefit, out of my bank account. (*He sighs*) It doesn't seem to go very far. The price of everything is quite alarming.

Mrs Martin I know, dear . . . when I do my baking tomorrow, I'll make you a big fruit cake and an apple tart. That'll help out.

James (*kindly but firmly*) No, Mum. Sorry old girl, but no. We're going to pay our way in this if it kills us. The cost of heating is the biggest expense we've got. I had to order a ton of coke last week and now we're putting aside all we can spare every week to pay the bill. I put it in the poor box in the front porch . . . the one with the rusty padlock. I've lost the key, so I know I won't be tempted to spend it.

Mrs Martin James dear, I hope you're not neglecting your chapel work.

James Oh, I think I'm keeping up with all the urgent matters. I mapped out next Sunday's sermon in my mind while waiting in the queue at Sainsbury's. Like to see what I bought, Mother? (*They delve into the basket*) That's some scrag end of lamb for a stew . . . onions . . . carrots . . . we'll have this for supper tonight when Julie gets home from work.

Sylvia From work? Julie's at work?

James (*pleased*) Started this morning. Waitress at the *Nightingale*. That should help the family finances.

Sylvia Yes. Then you won't need to bully her grandmother to give you her pension.

James Oh. Were you at the Post Office this morning?

Sylvia Yes, and so were half a dozen members of your congregation. It was a shocking scene, James. I felt terribly embarrassed. Taking an old woman's pension like that!

James (*with a rueful laugh*) Yes, it must have seemed pretty awful . . . but we needed the money to buy food. I'd already spent my share on some shoes and a skirt for Julie, so that she could look repectable when she went for her interview.

Sylvia All the same, you could have waited till the old lady got home.

James That's just the point. By the time she got home, it would be too late. She'd have spent the lot in the *Coach and Horses*.

Sylvia (*disgusted*) Oh, really!

James It's a fact. Poor old dear, she didn't like it when I said I'd come with her to draw her pension, but unless she toes the line, this family will never pay its way. (*He continues to unpack the basket*)

Pete (*coming forward*) Did you get my comic, Mr Martin?

James No, Pete, there wasn't enough money I'm afraid.

Pete Oh, sod it!

Mrs Martin (*horrified*) Oh!

James Never mind, Pete. Look, I popped into the library and got you a book about horses.

Pete (*pleased*) Oh, thanks. (*He takes the book and retires into the pulpit*)

James It was warm in the library. I was very much tempted to join the old age pensioners in the Reading Room. Do you realize how much fuel you can save by sitting in the library all morning? (*He has another spasm of coughing*)

Mrs Martin James dear, I hate to see you like this, struggling to keep warm, coughing your head off . . .

Act II, Scene 1

James (*feeling his chin*) Prickly as a hedgehog because Pete's busted my razor, and I haven't had a bath for a fortnight!
Sylvia (*shocked*) James!
James I do wash though. It's amazing how much you can cover with one kettle of water.
Mrs Martin There's a safety razor of your father's you can use ... or can't you even accept that?
James I think I'll have to. When I went into the bank they thought it was a hold-up! And on Sunday I'm preaching twice, so ... yes, please. I'll send Pete up for it this afternoon.
Mrs Martin All right. Goodbye then, dear, and do take care of yourself a bit better. Goodbye Sylvia.

Mrs Martin exits R

James (*coming downstage*) Well, darling, I haven't seen much of you lately, have I? What have you been doing with yourself?
Sylvia I've been going all over the town, trying in vain to find accommodation for the Briggs family.
James Have you really? That was kind of you.
Sylvia (*unhappily*) I wish it *was* kindness on my part, but it's not, James, and you know it's not. My sole desire is to put a stop to this situation.
James But we're doing all right, you know. We're getting our problems sorted out and Julie's got a job ...
Sylvia She can't support the four of you on a waitress's pay.
James I do contribute my share, you know. And tomorrow I'm taking Pete along to the Job Centre.
Sylvia He'll never hold down a job. It'll be one disappointment after another, James, and I can't bear to see you disillusioned.
James Disillusioned?
Sylvia When you find out what they're really like. You'll be so hurt.
James (*putting his arms round her*) You know, you're as bad as Julie. You think that because I'm a clergyman, I have to be shielded from reality. (*He kisses her*) Now stop worrying, love. Before very long Miss Pearson is sure to get them into a council flat and then I can stop playing let's pretend and go back to being a respectable clergyman again.
Sylvia You don't sound very pleased at the prospect.
James (*picking up the groceries and changing the subject*) I must put these away and think what we can rustle up for lunch.

Julie enters R, looking unusually clean and respectable in a dark skirt, new shoes and stockings, hair tied back

Julie (*with false gaiety*) Hallo, everyone, I'm back!
James Julie! I didn't think you'd be home for lunch!
Julie Well, I am you see, and I've brought some meat pasties for us. (*She hands James a paper bag*)
James Manna from heaven, and just in time for lunch. How did you get on? Are you exhausted? Sit down and rest while you can.
Julie (*throwing off her anorak and sitting*) Oh, my legs are killing me.

James (*hanging up her anorak*) How was it? Did you enjoy it?
Julie It was great. And guess what . . . I made ninety pence in tips! Where's our Pete?
Pete (*peering over the pulpit*) 'Ere.
Julie What yer doing in my bedroom? Come on down and I'll give you twenty pence.
Pete (*coming down*) Oh good, I'll be able to buy my comic.
Julie And I'll be able to buy some more tights. I've laddered these already. 'Ow d'you like my new shoes, Miss Grey?
Sylvia Very smart.
James Well, you won't have much time to spare so I'll go and get some plates and we'll have the pasties.
Julie Yes, let's. I'm starving. If Gran doesn't come, I'll 'ave 'er share too!

James exits R

Julie stops laughing and subsides dolefully on to a chair

Oh God!
Sylvia What's the matter?
Julie Can't you guess?
Sylvia You haven't . . . ?
Julie Yes, I 'ave. Got the push . . . the sack . . . got me cards . . . any way you like to put it.
Sylvia But you've only been there one morning. What went wrong?
Julie I was rude to the manageress. My blasted tongue! Why can't I keep my trap shut? Why must I always answer back?
Sylvia You're the limit, *really*! Three hours at work and you get the sack. You ought to be ashamed. (*After a pause*) Why haven't you told James the truth?
Julie 'Cos I'm scared.
Sylvia He won't be angry, you know.
Julie I know. That's just it. If only 'e'd shout and swear and 'it me, I wouldn't feel so bad about letting 'im down. But 'e won't. 'E'll understand and forgive me and encourage me to try again.
Sylvia (*wryly*) Yes, James has a sort of computer inside him and it's programmed to react to all kinds of human weakness with a forgiving smile instead of a kick in the pants.
Julie Oh, give me the kick in the pants every time. (*She stretches out her feet*) Look at these shoes and this skirt. 'E bought 'em for me, you know, so as I could look smart at my interview . . . and what do I reward 'im with? A bag of stolen meat pies!
Sylvia Stolen? You stole those meat pies?
Julie Yes, I was so mad with the manageress, as soon as she turned 'er back I nicked the first thing I could lay 'ands on.
Sylvia You're disgusting! You have no moral standards at all. (*After a pause*) Why have you told me? You didn't *have* to tell me.
Julie I dunno. I suppose because I knew I'd get a nice hard kick in the pants from you. You don't like me, do you?

Act II, Scene 1   35

Sylvia (*embarrassed*) There's nothing personal in it. It's people like you ... in a general sense ... that annoy me.
Julie I don't blame you. We can't seem to do anythink the right way. We always make a mess of it and 'ave to be got out of it by somebody else. Look, don't tell 'im, eh? I'll go out this afternoon and try and get another job. The shops'll be taking on extra staff for Christmas.
Sylvia Yes, "Burke and Harper" might take you on. But if you can't be polite they won't keep you.
Julie Oh, if only they'll give me another chance, I'll be like a dumb person, honest I will.

James enters R *carrying a tray with plates, meat pies and mugs of coffee*

James Here we are, meat pies and coffee. Staying to lunch, Sylvia?
Sylvia No thanks, I have to be at work by one o'clock. I'll have to hurry. (*She goes to the door*)
James Do look in again some time, darling. I don't seem to see much of you these days.
Sylvia (*beginning to smile*) No, you're too busy with your ... your family.
James Yes, I think there should be a society for the relief of unmarried fathers.
Sylvia It would never catch on. Bye, darling.

Sylvia gives James a quick kiss and exits

James lays out plates and pies. Pete sits eagerly and picks up a pie

James Not so fast. I haven't said grace.

Julie sits and bows her head. James does likewise

For what we are about to receive, may the Lord make us truly thankful.
Julie Amen.

They begin to eat

Where's Gran?
James Not yet back from the shops.
Julie I 'ope she's not at the pub.
James Can't be. She hasn't any money.
Julie 'Ave you saved 'er a pie?
James Of course.

They eat in silence for a moment

Pete (*conversationally*) Our Julie's got the sack.
Julie Pete!
Pete And she stole these pies.
Julie You bloody tell-tale!
James Is this true, Julie? Have you lost your job?
Julie (*sulkily*) Yes.
James And these pies were stolen?
Julie Yes.

James Then we can't eat them. (*He stands, takes away Julie's half-eaten pie and puts it on his plate. He holds out his hand for the remains of Pete's pie*) Give me your pie, Pete.
Pete Eh?
James It's stolen. You can't eat it.
Pete 'Oo says I can't?
James I do. Hand it over, mate.
Pete No bloody fear! (*He stuffs the pie into his mouth and edges away, expecting a blow*)
James I see. Well, the rest of us will have bread and cheese, but you won't need any since you're full of pie.

James exits R *with the pies*

Pete sits, chewing with some difficulty

Julie (*rising in wrath*) Bloody tell-tale! I 'ope it chokes yer! And don't think I'm giving you any pocket money after that. I wouldn't give you pocket money, not if you was dying! (*After a pause*) I know why you did it. You want Mr Martin to like you better 'n 'e likes me. It's just jealousy. And all you've done is make 'im 'ate us both. You wait till Gran comes 'ome. I'll tell 'er what 'appened to 'er nice meat pie, *and* 'ose fault it was!

Pete sinks lower in his seat. Julie turns away with her head in her hands

James enters with sliced bread, knife, margarine and cheese

James looks at them in silence, then spreads two slices of bread with margarine and puts a lump of cheese on each. He sets one beside Julie, on a plate

James (*in a matter of fact voice*) How did it happen then?
Julie What?
James Getting the sack. How did it happen?
Julie I was rude to the manageress.
James Why?
Julie Well, I didn't like the way she kept criticizing me.
James Oh. Have some bread and cheese?
Julie Thanks. (*She eats broodingly*)
James What did she say?
Julie 'Oo? The manageress?
James Yes. How did she criticize you?
Julie She said I was trying to go too fast. I slopped coffee in the saucers. She said I'd got to walk before I could run.
James And what did *you* say?
Julie (*defiantly*) I said, "I'm not a bleeding baby!"
James Hm. But you are, you know.
Julie What d'you mean?
James You take offence so easily. Grown-ups can usually take a bit of criticism. Especially if it's justified, as this was ... wasn't it?
Julie Well, what if it was? I wasn't going to let 'er start sitting on me. If you don't stick up for yourself, people think they can wipe their boots on you.

Act II, Scene 1   37

James That's not what it says in the Bible.
Julie Huh! The Bible! What do they know about it? (*She eats*) What *does* it say in the Bible?
James A soft answer turneth away wrath.
Julie Oh yeah, I know that one. Huh! Stupid idea. *You* do that, don't you? I've heard you lots of times. Well, I'm not like that, see? I don't give soft answers. I don't want people thinking *I'm* soft.
James Do you think *I'm* soft, then?
Julie (*grudgingly*) No. I thought so at first, but I changed my mind. You do a soft job but you must be quite tough underneath. Only ... you never get *angry* with people, do you? Don't you sometimes feel you'll burst if you bottle it all up inside you?
James No, I get my chance to let off steam every Sunday. If I wanted to, I could stand up in the pulpit and rave and threaten until they cowered in their seats.
Julie Smashing. I bet they ask for it, too.
James No. Their sins are so little and so very human. When I'm up there in the pulpit looking down at their mild, inoffensive faces, it's quite impossible to be angry with them.
Julie What do you preach about then, if you're not telling them off about their sins?
James (*walking about with his mug of coffee in his hand*) I usually take a story from the Bible and show how it still applies to life today. They listen very politely and try not to yawn, but I'm afraid it's awfully dull for them.
Julie Oh, go on!
James I'm afraid it is. I ... I don't preach awfully well. I suspect that a better preacher than I would have kept this chapel going. But my congregations tend to dwindle.
Julie But I always thought you'd be a lovely preacher.
James It's not easy, you know, to speak for about twenty minutes and keep it interesting.
Julie I bet *I* could do it.
Pete Garn, you never could!
Julie Yes I could. I'll show you. (*She jumps up*) Can I, Mr Martin? Can I go up there and preach?
James If you're serious. Not just making a joke of it.
Julie No, I'm not joking. I want to find out what it's like.
James Come on then, Pete. You and I will sit in the congregation and be preached at.
Pete Must I?
James It's either that or the washing up.

James moves down the steps and sits in the front row of the audience

Pete moves to sit on the steps. Julie mounts the pulpit and faces front, gripping the lectern

Julie Ladies and gentlemen ... is that all right?
James Very suitable.

Julie You seem a long way down.
James You seem a long way up.
Julie Well, it's right for people to look up at the preacher.
James I don't know. It cuts one off. Maybe in future I ought to stay on the ground.
Julie But you get a much better view up 'ere. You can see if the man in the back row is reading the prayer book or the "Racing News".
James My lot don't read the racing news. They go to sleep.
Pete 'Urry up and start, Julie. I'm getting a stiff neck.
Julie All right. I gotta gather my thoughts together. Mr Martin takes all the week to prepare 'is speech. (*After a pause*) Ladies and gentlemen, I want you all to consider your sins of the past week and repent of them before it's too late. Ah, yes, you're thinking you ain't got no sins, that you're all innocent and pure, sitting there in your best clothes and sucking peppermints. Well, all I can say is, think again! There's *you*, for instance, Mrs Parker. (*She looks accusingly at the audience*) You've got your fur coat on, I see. D'you know, Mrs Parker, that lots and lots of little animals ... pretty little 'armless animals ... was killed to make your fur coat? They 'ad a very short life, Mrs Parker. They'd 'ardly left their mother.
Pete (*very upset*) Oh Julie, don't talk about things like that! It's 'orrible.
Julie Shurrup! You're the congregation and you can't answer back. Repent, Mrs Parker! Give your coat to Oxfam and you'll sleep easy at night. (*She looks round the audience*) And what about you, Mr Pringle? You think you're a respectable butcher, just 'cos you've got a collecting box for the blind on your counter ... but what about them chickens you sell, what never see the light of day? You ought to be ashamed, selling chickens what 'ave bin reared in captivity like a lot of prisoners, in smelly little boxes!
Pete Mr Martin, make 'er stop it!
Julie Am I doing all right, Mr Martin?
James Splendid. I doubt if John Wesley could have done any better. How long can you keep it up?
Julie Hours. I 'aven't got started yet. I'd like to ask *you*, Mrs Mackintosh, 'ow you feel about your poor old father, what you 'ad put into an old people's 'ome because 'e was such a nuisance. 'E was deaf and 'e talked to 'imself when you 'ad visitors and 'e spilled 'is food down 'is front and made you ashamed, so you 'ad 'im put away. You're a wicked woman and I 'ope that when you're old, someone'll do the same to you.
Pete Mr Martin, I don't like it.
Julie You ain't *meant* to like it, is 'e Mr Martin?
James Well, it's splendid stuff but it's all rather harrowing, isn't it?
Julie 'Arrowing? Well, they need 'arrowing. That's what they come to church for.
James Do you really think so?
Julie Course it is. Now, where's Mr Banks? (*She peers across the audience*) Ah, I can see you, Mr Banks. Don't you look smart and good, as if butter wouldn't melt in your mouth? Your wife looks tired, Mr Banks. It must be because she works in the 'ospital every evening. Does she know what

Act II, Scene 1

you do while she's out at work? Does she know you've been 'aving it off with the neighbour while 'er back's turned?

James covers his face with one hand

Does she know the baby screams 'isself sick while you're next door enjoying yourself? You'd better repent, Mr Banks, and 'urry up about it, or one of these days, the Devil's going to get you! (*She pauses and grins*) I'm enjoying this, you know.
James You certainly have a personal touch. If ever you took holy orders, you'd really ginger things up.
Julie I don't know why you say it's difficult. Up 'ere in the pulpit, you feel just like God.
James I know. Up there you think you're giving the sermon of your life. It's only when you come down to earth you realize that it wasn't.

There is a sound of singing, off stage, at the back of the hall

Julie 'Oo's that singing?
Pete (*standing up*) It's our Gran! She's tight!
James She can't be!

They all face the back of the hall

Gran enters at the back of the hall, drunk, singing "My Old Man Said Follow the Van"

Julie She is! She's drunk as a fiddler's bitch!
James But where did she get the money from? She only had fivepence when I left her.
Pete She come back 'ere after that and got some money.
James Where from?
Pete (*pointing to the back of hall*) Out there, I think.
James The poor box!

He runs down the aisle, dodging Gran, and exits at the back

Julie moves down off stage and meets Gran at the foot of the steps

Julie (*off*) Gran, you're awful! You're pissed again! Where did you get the money?

Gran sings

Stop that racket, you 'orrible old sod. 'Ere. Pete, 'elp me get 'er up the steps.

The three of them struggle up on to the stage

James enters at the back of the hall

James She's broken open the poor box! She's taken all our savings! Every penny gone on gin! (*He sounds more amazed than angry*)
Julie (*shattered*) Gran! You stole our savings and boozed the lot! 'Ow could you do such a terrible thing?

Gran I'm a wicked old woman.
Julie Yes you are. Wicked as 'ell.

James moves forward, up the steps and on to the stage

Gran I'm a wicked old woman. (*She sees James and staggers to grab his arm*) Mr Martin, I'm a wicked old woman. I stole your savings. I must make my confession. Shall I kneel down?
James (*trying to hold her up*) No, no.
Julie Gran, stop it!
Gran (*sliding to her knees*) Yes, you got to kneel down when you confess and I want to confess to the 'oly father.
Julie 'E's not that kind of 'oly father, you stupid nit!
Gran I took the money, your 'oliness, 'cos I wanted a drink. I wanted it so bad, as if I'd bin dry for a year. 'Ave you ever 'ad such a terrible thirst, yer 'oliness? I don't suppose you 'ave so I'll get no sympathy from you.
Julie (*bursting into tears*) Gran, don't talk like that!
Gran It was a bugger to open, that poor box was. I 'ad to get the poker to it.
Julie I wish I could get the poker to you! Can't you see what we're doing to 'im? All we ever do is let 'im down!

Julie runs out R, *weeping*

James supports Gran to two chairs and they sit side by side, Gran, still singing, leans drunkenly on James

Gran All things bright and beautiful,
All creatures great and small,
James (*joining in lustily*)
All things wise and wonderful,
The Lord God made them all.

They continue to sing as——

——the CURTAIN *falls*

SCENE 2

The same. Saturday afternoon, a week later

James is sitting at the table, working at his sermon. Julie is perched on the pulpit steps, laboriously sewing a button on her anorak. There is a copy of the Methodist Recorder *on the table. James bites his pen, frowns, then puts it down and picks up the paper*

Julie Something good in the paper?
James (*hardly attending*) Mm?
Julie I said, is there something good in the paper?
James Er ... no. It's just the *Methodist Recorder*. It's never very exciting.
Julie It can't be *that* dull. You've 'ad your nose glued to it for most of the afternoon. (*After a pause*) 'Ave you finished your sermon?

Act II, Scene 2   41

James (*putting aside his paper*) No . . . I don't seem to make much progress.
Julie I know. I bin watching you. You've written 'arf a page and then crossed it out again.
James (*standing up*) I can't seem to concentrate. What are *you* doing?
Julie Sewing a button on my anorak. Got to look respectable when I start my new job next week.
James (*vaguely*) Yes. (*He stands lost in thought*)
Julie Your sweetheart gave me the needle and cotton. She said my anorak was a downright disgrace.
James Oh . . . Sylvia's a bit outspoken . . .
Julie I didn't take offence. I thought it was nice of 'er to bother 'ow I looked.

James goes back to his newspaper

It reminded me of our mum. She used to talk like that. A bit sharp, but you din't mind 'cos it was just 'er way. "Julie!" she'd say, "Comb yer 'air, you look just like an old lavatory brush!" (*After a pause*) You're not listening, are you?
James (*putting down his paper*) I'm sorry, Julie. What were you saying?
Julie I was saying that my mum and your sweetheart was tarred with the same brush.
James How d'you mean?
Julie Like you said, outspoken. No white lies. Tell you the truth even if it 'urts like 'ell. Difficult sort of people, but all right when you get to know them better.
James And you're getting to know Sylvia better now?
Julie Sort of.

Gran enters R *with a tin of sardines*

Gran Julie! I can't find the key to this sardine tin. 'Ave you seen it?
Julie (*coming down the pulpit steps*) It must 'ave fell out. It'll be at the bottom of the basket, I expect.
Gran Can you come and 'ave a look for it?

Julie exits R

Gran begins to follow but James calls her back

James Gran!
Gran What?
James You've been avoiding me.
Gran I don't know what you mean.
James I mean that as soon as I come in you slide out of the door, you haven't addressed two words to me for nearly a week and you won't even look me in the eye.
Gran (*very embarrassed*) I can't.
James Can't look me in the eye? Why not?
Gran 'Cos of what I done.
James When?

Gran Last Tuesday.
James Oh. You mean when you ... got a bit tipsy.
Gran Yes.
James Ah well, what's a bit of foolishness between friends?
Gran Julie told me what I said. I said awful things. She went on at me somethink cruel and I'm not surprised. I stole your money.
James Our money.
Gran Our money then, wot you'd tried so 'ard to save, and now we can't afford to pay for any coal.
James Well, we're not due to pay for a few more weeks, so we'll have time to save a bit if we're very careful.
Gran Next time I go and draw my pension, you better come with me and I'll 'and over the lot without a murmur.
James That's the spirit. Now don't let's dwell on past errors. When's teatime? I'm thirsty.
Gran As soon as I can open these 'ere sardines and make some sandwiches.
James Sardine sandwiches for tea? What are we celebrating?
Gran Julie's birthday, of course.
James It's really Julie's birthday? Today?
Gran Yeh. Really.
James Why on earth didn't someone tell me? I must go and get her something. Have we got a birthday cake?
Gran (*ruefully*) Some 'ope!
James I'll get one.
Gran They'll all be gone by now. It's nearly five o'clock.
James (*going*) I'll get something. Don't tell her. We must have a proper celebration.

He rushes down the hall, bumping into Sylvia as she enters. She is carrying a handbag

Sylvia Where are you going?
James To get a cake. It's Julie's birthday.
Sylvia Oh, not again. I don't believe it.
James This time it's true.

James exits at the rear of the hall

Sylvia (*going up on stage; to Gran*) Is it?
Gran Well, I think so. It's either today or yesterday.

Julie enters R

Julie, it *is* your birthday today, innit?
Julie Yeh. Course it is. 'Ere, Gran I can't find no sardine key. You must 'ave lost it.
Gran Well, 'ow am I supposed to open the bloody thing without a key?
Sylvia Let me look at it. Yes, I thought so. It's the new sort of tin. You just pull this ring ... you see ... and it opens.
Gran Well! I never saw one like that before. Thanks, Miss Grey. You better stay to tea.

Act II, Scene 2 43

Gran exits R

Sylvia Well, I'm not sure if I ...
Julie (*urgently*) Miss Grey, where is Mr Martin?
Sylvia Er ... he just slipped out.
Julie Good. I want to show you something.
Sylvia Show me what?
Julie Something in the paper. I'm very worried about it. Look!
Sylvia (*taking the paper from her*) This bit with the red ring round it?
Julie Yes. 'E keeps on reading it, over and over again.
Sylvia (*reading aloud*) "Are you young, tough and practical? The Brightwater Mission, Southwell, urgently needs a third man to help run this challenging project in the heart of London's dockland. One year only, starting January 1st. Must be single and live in. Ring after six o'clock." (*She stares at Julie*) You say that James keeps reading this?
Julie Yes. 'E drew that ring round it. And 'e's bin ever so absent minded for three days now. Always in a kind of dream. 'Ardly listens when you speak to 'im.
Sylvia Are you seriously suggesting that James wants this job?
Julie I dunno. What d'you think?
Sylvia It's ridiculous. He wouldn't leave us ... me and his mother ... you and your family? Of course he wouldn't. (*After a pause*) When did this paper come out?
Julie Thursday I think. 'E was very quiet all afternoon and straight after six o'clock 'e picked up the paper and went across to the phone booth. 'E was in there for a quarter of an hour. I watched 'im from the front porch.
Sylvia You're jumping to conclusions. He may happen to know someone who would like the job. A friend.
Julie Would that explain 'im going off into a dream and biting 'is nails and looking worried?
Sylvia That could be because he's writing his sermon. He always bites his nails when he's ... oh!
Julie What's up?
Sylvia I've got a letter for him. (*She takes a long manila envelope out of her bag*) I met his mother and she asked me to give it to him. It came this morning.
Julie Can you read the post mark?
Sylvia (*after a moment's study*) Southwell!
Julie Oh gawd!
Sylvia Now, don't look as if the bottom had fallen out of things. It could be something he's needing for a sermon.
Julie You mean ... per'aps 'e's going to preach about this place ... wot's it called?
Sylvia The Brightwater Mission. It's some sort of evangelist affair in a particularly crummy part of London. Nobody in their right mind would *want* to go there and live.
Julie 'Ow can we find out?
Sylvia I shall ask him of course. You'd better leave us alone when he comes back.

Julie But you'll tell me wot 'e says? I gotta know.
Sylvia Yes, we've both "gotta know", haven't we?
Julie Look out, 'e's coming.

James enters at the back of the hall, with a cake in a bag

James (*advancing on to the stage*) Happy Birthday, Julie. I just heard the news. Here's something for the birthday tea.
Julie Thanks, Mr Martin. Shall I take it out to Gran?
James Yes, do.

Julie exits R

Darling, I'm glad you've come. There's something I want to talk to you about.
Sylvia (*picking up the paper*) It wouldn't be this, by any chance?
James (*a bit nonplussed*) Well ... yes. How did you know?
Sylvia Julie guessed. She says you keep staring at it. James, are you going to tell me that you want this job?
James (*gravely*) Yes.

She stares at him

Oh Sylvia, don't look at me like that.
Sylvia Like what?
James Well ... baffled.
Sylvia I *am* baffled. I would have thought you had everything a man of your calling could wish for.
James No. I haven't. For years now I've felt a vague discontent. I entered the church full of high ideals. I wanted to fight against wrong. I was eager to come to grips with untold difficulties ... but I never meet any worth speaking of.
Sylvia Oh come ...
James It's true, Sylvia. I'm thirty years old, in excellent health, I have good muscles and good nerves. I'm incorruptably honest, I can stand up to shock, privation and hardship. When are these qualities ever called upon? Up till a few weeks ago I was hardly aware that I had any hidden qualities, but thank God, the arrival of the Briggs family woke me up. It's been the most satisfying time of my life ... and there are hundreds of people like the Briggs. I want to help them, Sylvia.
Sylvia At the Brightwater Mission?
James Why not? There's vice there, prostitution, racism, drug trafficking, crimes that would make Gran and Julie look like shining angels. I want to be there, in the thick of it, fighting with everything I've got.
Sylvia Even if it means abandoning the Briggs'? How can you be so selfish, James? Maybe you *have* got a talent for this sort of work. Maybe you could fill the post very adequately ... but you can't leave Julie and Pete and Gran with their problems unsolved. You took them in and made yourself indispensable to them. How can you walk out on them, now you've found someone who needs you more?

Act II, Scene 2

James That's just it. They *do* need me more. To me, that advertisement is like a trumpet call and I'd be failing in my duty to ignore it.
Sylvia Your duty lies *here*, James. It's arrogant to assume that Julie's needs are less important, just because you want to try your strength on something bigger. (*After a pause*) Have you given yourself time to think?
James I've thought of nothing else for three days. I want it more than anything else in the world.
Sylvia (*with difficulty*) More than you want me?
James (*after a moment*) Must I lose you, darling?
Sylvia I can't come with you. It says you must be single.
James It's only for a year. We could be married when the year's up.
Sylvia And come back here?
James I don't know. My darling, I just don't know. But wherever I go, I shall want you to be there.

She goes and clings to him, very unhappy

We're rather overlooking one thing.
Sylvia What's that?
James I might not be offered the job.
Sylvia There's a letter for you. It has the Southwell postmark. (*She gets it for him*)
James When did this come?
Sylvia This morning I suppose. Your mother gave it me when we met at the shops. Aren't you going to open it?
James I suppose I'd better. There's no point in upsetting everyone if this is to turn me down. I think I'll go down the end and read it in a quiet corner. (*He turns to go, then looks back*) You're right, of course. I've got to think of Julie and her family. I can't just ditch them, can I? They're so helpless.

James goes down the steps to the back of the hall

Julie creeps in R

Julie 'E's going to do it, ain't 'e? 'E's going to ditch us both.
Sylvia You heard?
Julie Yeh. It's easy to over'ear things in this place. What are we going to do?
Sylvia We must fight to keep him. *You* must fight, Julie. Tell him you need him. Tell him Gran will get drunk and Pete will run away and Mr Brown will break in at night ...
Julie 'E can't do that. Mr Martin 'ad the lock changed. And Gran's promised to be good and I've got a new job and ... well, the fact is, we don't need 'im arf as much as those 'orrible people at the Mission, do we? 'E says we're like angels compared to them.
Sylvia He cares more about leaving you than he does about leaving me. He thinks he can go off for a year and then come back and pick up where we left off. It's not fair.
Julie No, it ain't. I think it's rotten luck, you expecting to get married and then ... this 'appens. But it's amazing 'ow quickly a year goes by, and then you'll be fixing the 'appy day.

Sylvia (*bitterly*) Will we?
Julie Mr Martin would never break a promise.
Sylvia He'll be different, once he's lived that kind of life. It'll change him, I know it will.
Julie Then you'll 'ave to change too.
Sylvia I can't, Julie. I can't.
Julie Yes, you can. If you love 'im you can.
Sylvia I don't want to live in places like that. I want to stay here, in Willowby.
Julie I know. But 'e doesn't. And if you try to keep 'im you'll lose 'im.
Sylvia I realize that. But *you* could make him stay. He couldn't turn his back on *you*, Julie, if you said you needed him.
Julie I can't do it, Miss Grey. You 'eard what 'e said. 'E wants this job more than anything else in the world. I think 'e's mad. As if life ain't difficult enough, 'e wants bigger problems, worse difficulties. 'E's potty, but I'm not going to stand in 'is way.

Gran enters R *with a tray of saucers and cups and a table-cloth*

Gran Wheres our Pete? I ain't seen 'im all afternoon and now it's tea-time.
Julie I 'ope 'e won't be late for my birthday tea.
Gran 'E's probably forgotten.

Gran exits R, *leaving the tray*

Julie begins to lay the table

James comes back on to the stage

James I'm invited to go for an interview.
Sylvia When?
James The day after tomorrow. They . . . they haven't yet offered me the job but it sounds as though I'm the likeliest candidate.
Sylvia Surely you couldn't just *go*, in a matter of weeks? You have a parish here depending on you.
James They'd arrange for a locum. A retired minister, living nearby perhaps. No, that's no trouble, and Mother won't object. The only thing that worries me is leaving you two girls.
Julie Oh, you don't need to worry about *me*, Mr Martin. I've got some good news from Miss Pearson. Now I'm eighteen I can 'ave a council flat in my own name and there's one coming vacant soon after Christmas.
James (*delighted*) Julie! That's marvellous! Why didn't you tell me?
Julie I was saving it up, till tea-time.
James Sylvia, isn't that wonderful?
Sylvia It would be, if it were true.
James It's not true?
Sylvia Of course it isn't true. I saw Miss Pearson this afternoon and she says that with their record they stand no chance at all.
Julie (*in quiet fury*) You bitch! You stupid, stupid bitch! Why couldn't you keep your mouth shut, just for once?
Sylvia Because it's no good telling lies to get James off the hook.

Act II, Scene 2

Julie Nobody asked *you* to tell lies! If I want to tell a thumping great lie to 'elp Mr Martin, what right 'ave you to interfere?
Sylvia Julie, listen. if he goes, he should go knowing what he leaves behind—a family of helpless, immoral nitwits who can't control their own lives without someone in charge to guide them, day and night. James is the only thing that has kept this family together. Surely you know that.
James You mean . . . if I go away, they'll be split up and sent into care?
Julie Oh gawd! They wouldn't do that, would they? Would they, Miss Grey?

Gran brings in a plate of sandwiches and the cake, puts them on the table and exits R

Sylvia Julie, how long before your father comes out of prison?
Julie Five more months. (*She looks at James in horror and speaks almost in a whisper*) They musn't split us up. I promised our dad.

James sits despondently, head in hands

Gran enters R, *with a large teapot*

Gran 'Ere, I made the tea. 'Ow long do we wait for our Pete?

Nobody answers

Julie Miss Grey . . . this means 'e won't go, dunnit? I expect you'll be glad.

Sylvia turns away

Oh Lord, we 'ad to be the fly in the ointment, didn't we? I'm sorry, Mr Martin. Couldn't they wait five months for you, just until my dad comes 'ome?
James (*sadly*) No, Julie. The post must be filled by the New Year.
Gran 'Ere, cheer up. It's Julie's birthday. Come and sit at the table.

Pete enters R

'Ullo, 'ere's our Pete. Just in time. Where you bin?
Pete Down the village.
Gran Well, sit down and 'ave a sandwich.
Pete Wot's in em? (*He lifts the bread and looks inside*)
Gran Sardines. You can 'ave two each. I cut 'em nice and thick.

They all sit at the table. James pours out cups of tea and passes them round. Gran passes round the sandwiches

Whenever I 'ave sardines I think of VE Day. We 'ad a party in the street for the kids and everyone wore paper 'ats and all the mothers brought something special to eat, whatever they could spare from their rations. I'd bin saving up this tin of sardines for *years* and it 'ad got a bit rusty but I thought it smelled all right so I made a pile of sandwiches. Only nobody et any of 'em. In the end I et 'em all meself. I was as sick as a dog that night. I shall always remember them sardines.

Sound of cows mooing

Theodore Brown runs in R, *distraught*

Brown Mr Martin! Mr Martin, come quick! The graveyard's full of cows!
James (*leaping up*) Cows?
Brown Yes, cows everywhere, stamping all over Dora's grave. And the bull's loose, too!
James Oh no! Not the bull!
Brown (*pointing at Pete*) It's all his fault. It's that gormless Briggs boy let them out.

Julie runs up into the pulpit, to see out of the window

Julie It's true! There's cows all over the place. 'Undreds of 'em!

Pete makes a dash for the door but James gets there first and confronts him

James Pete, is this true? Did you let them out?
Pete (*stammering*) I did like St Francis. 'E went up and down the country setting the animals free. Mrs Martin said 'e did. So I set free Mr Pike's cows.
Brown I told you so. The boy's insane.
Julie No 'e ain't. 'E's just soft-'earted.
Pete Only I don't think it was a very good idea. They might 'ave an accident on the main road.
Brown I very nearly did have an accident. I turned out of my gateway and there was this ... this oaf, wandering up the middle of the street with the bull breathing down his neck like any tame pony. I nearly dropped dead with fright.
Pete I don't know why they followed me 'ere. I never meant 'em to. I didn't know what to do, so I ... I come in and 'ad me tea.
Brown Mr Martin, can't you do something?
James (*chortling*) Me? I'm only trained as a shepherd.
Brown But Dora's grave ...
Sylvia (*kindly but with authority*) Pete. If they followed you here, they would follow you home again. I think you had better try.
Pete Take 'em back?
Sylvia Yes. Round them up and take them back to Farmer Pike. They're your responsibility, you know. You can't just come indoors and have your tea.
Pete (*seeing the force of this argument*) Oh. Will you come too, Mr Martin?
James All right Pete ... but you'll have to handle the bull.
Pete Can I 'ave my bit of birthday cake first?

As Gran cuts his cake and he eats it, Brown addresses James and Sylvia

Brown How much longer have we got to put up with this sort of thing, I want to know?
James The Briggs family will be here for another five months, Mr Brown. We must be prepared for anything, it seems.
Brown Well, I just hope that you can cope with them, Mr Martin.
Sylvia Mr Martin may not be here.

Act II, Scene 2

Brown Not here?
Sylvia I said he *may* not. But if he should be called away, you have no need to worry. I shall be able to cope.
Julie (*looking out of the window*) Cripes! Mr Brown, you should see what the bull's done on your wife's grave!
Brown What? On Dora's ... quick! Young Briggs, stop stuffing your mouth and get out there! Come on, Mr Martin, there's not a second to lose!

Brown exits R propelling Pete in front of him

James (*half going but turning back*) Sylvia ... what did you mean?
Sylvia Darling, the bull ...
James Hang the bull. I must know what you meant. When you said that I might be called away ... after that ...
Sylvia I seem to remember saying that I could cope.
James Did you mean it?
Sylvia (*half surprised at herself*) I suppose I must have.
Julie You mean, look after us, sort of?
Sylvia Why not? I know I said you needed someone in charge, day and night, but I didn't say it had to be James, did I?
James Sylvia! You don't mean, you'd take over for me?
Sylvia Don't you think I could do it? I have a few hidden qualities too ... remember? You said I was strong-minded, domineering and upright as a telegraph pole. That should see us through the next five months with luck. And if ever I'm going to marry the sort of man who goes looking for trouble, I think it's time I put in a bit of practice.
James (*hugging her*) Oh, you wonderful girl! I don't deserve you!

Brown looks round the door in desperation

Brown Mr Martin!
James Coming!

Brown disappears from view

Wait here, darling. As soon as I've rounded up the stragglers I'm coming back to say thank you properly.

James gives her a smacking kiss and rushes out R

Sylvia (*ruefully smiling*) It looks as though I shall be doing that for the rest of my life.
Julie Doing what?
Sylvia Waiting for James to round up the stragglers.

Gran sits and gets on with her tea

Have you got a good view up there?
Julie Great. Come on up.

Sylvia mounts the stairs of the pulpit

You was a brick, Miss Grey, to say you'd take us on. I 'ope we don't let you down.

Sylvia If you do, you know what you'll get.
Julie
Sylvia } (*together grinning*) A kick in the pants.

Sylvia puts her arm round Julie's shoulders and they look out of the window laughing

CURTAIN

FURNITURE AND PROPERTY LIST

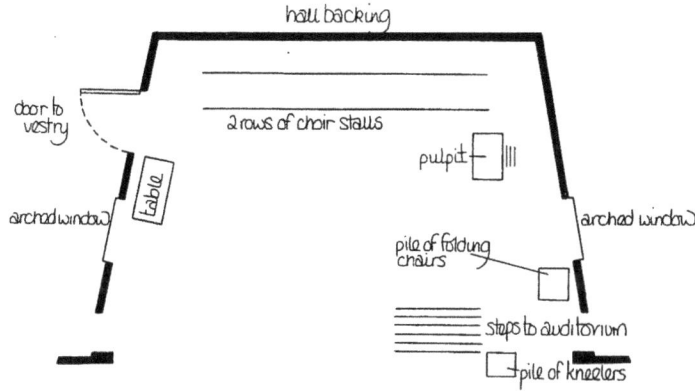

ACT I

Scene 1

On stage: Table. *On it:* small pile of old hymn books, half a bottle of milk, battered packet of cornflakes
3 folding chairs
36 kneelers on floor of auditorium
Battered suitcase behind pulpit
Shoe box for "guinea-pig"

Personal: **Sylvia:** shopping bag
Miss Pearson: briefcase

Scene 2

Set: 2 chairs
Table. *On it:* 2 mugs of tea, small Calor gas type camping stove with a kettle on it, remains of a meal, plates, cutlery
Shoe box behind pulpit
Anorak on choir stalls
Suitcase behind pulpit. *In it:* pair of pyjamas, 2 nightdresses, comb, towel

Offstage: Red roadside lantern **(James)**
2 blankets, 2 sleeping-bags, 2 sheets, 1 rubber groundsheet **(Pete)**

Personal: **Pete:** mug of tea
James: 2 electric light bulbs, key of back door

ACT II

Scene 1

Strike: Kneelers, bedding, lantern

Set: Table and 2 chairs c
Chair down L
Clothes line with sheets
Poster on pulpit
Towels on pulpit

Off stage: Tray with plates, cutlery, pasties, mugs of coffee **(James)**
Tray with sliced bread, margarine, cheese and a knife **(James)**

Personal: **Pete:** hammer and nails
Mrs Martin: umbrella
James: shopping basket with food and library book, jacket
Julie: paper bag with 4 pasties, anorak, dark skirt, new shoes and stockings, ribbon in hair

Scene 2

Strike: Clothes line and sheets

Set: Table and 2 chairs c. *On table:* copy of *Methodist Recorder*, **James's** sermon
1 chair down L
2 chairs behind pulpit

Offstage: Birthday cake in a bag **(James)**
Tray with cups, saucers, cutlery, table-cloth **(Gran)**
Plate of sandwiches and birthday cake **(Gran)**
Large teapot **(Gran)**

Personal: **Julie:** anorak, needles, thread, button
James: pen
Gran: tin of sardines, ring-pull type
Sylvia: handbag containing a long, manila envelope

LIGHTING PLOT

Practical fittings required: 2 light sockets minus bulbs

Interior. A Methodist Chapel. The same scene throughout

ACT I, SCENE 1

To open: Cold morning light

No cues

ACT I, SCENE 2

To open: Dim twilight

Cue 1	As **James** switches on the lights *Bring lights to medium bright*	(Page 16)
Cue 2	**Pete:** "Yeah." **James** puts out the lights *Dim lights. Stage to be lit by red glow only*	(Page 28)

ACT II, SCENE 1

To open: Cold morning light

No cues

ACT II, SCENE 2

To open: Afternoon light

EFFECTS PLOT

ACT I

No cues

ACT II

Cue 1   **Gran:** "I shall always remember them sardines."   (Page 47)
          Sound of cows mooing. Continue to end of scene

www.ingramcontent.com/pod-product-compliance
Ingram Content Group UK Ltd.
Pitfield, Milton Keynes, MK11 3LW, UK
UKHW021847210426
5322IPUK00022B/527